B E H O L D

EXPERIENCE A LIFESTYLE OF INTIMACY WITH YOUR CREATOR.

BRICE TABOR

Tabor

PUBLISHING

BEHOLD
© Copyright 2019 Brice Tabor, Tabor Publishing
www.taborpublishing.com

ISBN 978-0-578-48243-9

DEDICATION

This book is dedicated to my wife, Jessica. Thank you for your servant's heart and all the sacrifices you have made in our journey together. You display such humility and trust as we seek to do what pleases the Lord.

Special thanks to Vicki Tabor, Christie Tabor, and Christie Fruits for the hours and hours of editing that were put into this book.

WHAT OTHERS ARE SAYING

"Who better to write a book about worship than Brice Tabor! He is a worship leader and devoted lover of God. *BEHOLD* will leave you stunned as you open your heart to these divine gems of truth about worship that will challenge and change you. As you go through these chapters, you'll learn about worship through a new lens – beholding the One you love. If you *behold* long enough, you'll *become* even more like Jesus! Enjoy this book and get one for a friend!"

Dr. Brian Simmons
Lead Translator of The Passion Translation (TPT) | Passion & Fire Ministries

"*BEHOLD* is a wonderful book on intimacy with God. This is the one thing that must remain of paramount importance for every believer. We become what we gaze at and consume. This is why Jesus said, "Unless you eat my flesh and drink my blood, you have no life within you." We were made by God and for God. Any other agenda or lifestyle will leave us empty and disappointed. The flow of God's life and love makes us emotionally sound, physically healthy, and mentally sharp so that we can be overcomers in this world. Consume this book and *behold* your God."

Joan Hunter
Author/Evangelist | Host of "Miracles Happen!"

"Brice Tabor has a unique ability to lead people into a deep worship experience. I have had the privilege of experiencing this at his church in Wichita, Kansas. As I read through *BEHOLD*, it becomes obvious to me why I had such a profound experience. This book shares his experiences, the biblical truths he has discovered, and the practical steps he has learned which have created this impactful worship. You will be inspired and led into deeper worship through *BEHOLD*, but, more importantly, you will be given keys that will dramatically affect your spiritual life, especially your secret times with Jesus. I highly recommend this book."

Steve Backlund
Pastor at Bethel Church, Redding, CA | Igniting Hope Ministries

"Brice Tabor's *BEHOLD* is a book that brought the WOW out of me. His insights on how to help us see Jesus in our spirit are life-changing. As a person who was given the grace to behold Jesus in a heavenly way, I can say that reading this book will help you learn how to see Jesus in a pure way and know he is your Lord and Savior. *BEHOLD* will take you on a journey to experience Christ in a deeper way every time you desire. Brice accomplishes this in detail - explaining profound differences between worship in flesh and spirit. He not only wants people to know of Jesus but also to be awakened to the knowledge of God by seeing him. I believe you will be changed and begin to behold Jesus as he is by reading this book."

Dean Braxton
Author/Speaker | Dean Braxton Ministries

TABLE OF CONTENTS

Here's the one thing I crave from God,
the one thing I seek above all else:
I want the privilege of living with him every
moment in his house, finding the sweet
loveliness of his face, filled with awe,
delighting in his glory and grace.

PSALM 27:4 (TPT)

FOREWORD

I have known Brice Tabor all of his life. I have had the wonderful blessing of watching him grow into the man he is today. Brice is the youngest of our four children. In his teenage years, Brice's desire for worship led him to teach himself the guitar and to sing and play privately in the Lord's presence. In John 4, Jesus tells the Samaritan woman,

> *But the hour is coming, and now is, when the true worshipers will worship the Father in spirit and truth; for the Father is seeking such to worship Him. God is Spirit, and those who worship Him must worship in spirit and truth. (John 4:23-24, NKJV)*

The Father is seeking such to worship him. To think that God "seeks" or goes after this type of person! This is the journey that Brice has been on and continues to travel. Worship to Brice goes beyond playing music and singing beautifully scripted songs. It is about connecting heart-to-heart with the Lord. Jesus said in John 17:3 (NKJV), "And this is eternal life, that they may know You, the only true God, and Jesus Christ whom You have sent."

Jesus is expressing true intimacy with God. He is speaking of experiencing true connection with God. A real relational encounter with the living God. This is a heart of worship. This type of encounter with the Lord is what Brice has demonstrated in his life and seeks to lead others in.

The word "behold" is a beautiful word. It expresses, "stop and look" and "pause with expectation." One dictionary defines it as, "observe," and better yet, "feast your eyes upon." That paints a great picture.

The word "selah" in the Hebrew is used to tell the reader to stop and pause, take time to reflect, and meditate upon. This is the essence of this book. It is written to encourage and challenge people into a close, intimate relationship with God the Father. It is an invitation to abandon fears and false speculations about God's character. It welcomes us to enter into God's loving embrace and behold him.

This is the type of call to worship that Brice leads our congregation into at New Life Covenant Church. This open transparency of worship is not something you can teach through steps. It is arrived at only through spending time in the Lord's presence.

BEHOLD is written by a man who has encountered the living Christ and has been so impacted by those encounters that he wants everyone to know and experience the King of kings. Brice understands what it is like to wash the Lord's feet with his tears and has also had his own feet washed by the Master.

Through his times of worship, he, like the woman at the well, says to those around him, "Come see a man who told me everything about my life." His worship has touched the heart of God, and each week he leads others in corporate worship to touch God's heart. It is his desire to help others connect with excitement and wonder, the supernatural experience similar to what the first disciples who visited the empty tomb might have felt. The feeling that makes us want to say, "He is risen and is alive - come and see." Jesus is alive and we *have* seen him. Come and see. It is well worth the journey. Psalm 27:4 (NKJV) says, "One thing I have desired of the Lord, that will I seek: That I may dwell in the house of the Lord all the days of my life, to behold the beauty of the Lord, and to inquire in His temple."

Brice's humble heart and attitude have prompted him by the leading of the Holy Spirit to write this book to encourage others to go deeper and step out and behold the Lord.

Kit Tabor
Senior Pastor | New Life Covenant Church

INTRODUCTION

I've been praying for you.

As I wrote this book, many tears streamed down my face at the dream of readers like you experiencing the joys of knowing Jesus more intimately. I've been asking the Lord to bring freedom into your life like you have never known before. I've prayed that the eyes of your understanding would be opened to the divine opportunity that lies before you each moment of every day. I hope that you will more regularly experience the bliss and pleasures of knowing Jesus Christ through the indwelling presence of the Holy Spirit. I believe he has heard my heart's cries.

I'm very excited for you. You are seeking him, and he is a rewarder of those who diligently seek him. I'm expecting that as you read, the Holy Spirit will reveal himself to you and transform you just like he did to me. What he has taught me in regards to time with God has completely changed my life, and I believe he assigned me to share the truths in this book to help you. As over-the-top as that might sound, I really do believe it.

This book is meant to be interactive. It's an invitation to experience the delight of nearness to your Creator in a more intimate way than you've ever known. I urge you to not read through the content just as knowledge to be gained, but rather as an opportunity to develop a closer friendship with God that you routinely engage in.

At the end of each chapter, there are reflection questions and an empty page. The purpose of the reflection questions is to help you process what you've learned and how it applies to your life. The empty page after the questions is there for you to dream in the Spirit. Expect the Holy Spirit to give you thoughts from his heart, and when he does, use that space to express it. If you like to write, then write it out. If you like to draw, then go for it. Don't worry about what it looks like. It's between you and the Lord. Let your heart and soul run wild with the Holy Spirit. Dream, believe, and know that the Holy Spirit is at work in you.

CHAPTER 1

THE STRUGGLE

I'm a PK.

For those who don't know, that's short for "pastor's kid."
When I tell people I'm a PK I usually get a response like,
"Oh, so you were a really bad kid growing up!" But that
wasn't necessarily the case for me.

I went through some seasons of bad choices. The
person I was in church didn't line up with the person I was
outside of church. I hung out with the popular crowd in
the public school system so I was constantly torn between
the pull of living the world's way and the pull of living for
God.

But I never "went off the deep end," as some put it.
I never set out to pursue the desires of the flesh completely
apart from God. I grew up in a home with grounded, Biblical

principles. Principles that were helpful and not just rigid rules to follow. The focus was love and the heart of the matter. It was never about performance.

My parents weren't perfect, but no parents are. They did a phenomenal job raising me. When my siblings or I made mistakes, we would get a healthy dose of discipline but it was done in love. And if my parents ever stepped outside of love, they were always quick to admit their fault and apologize. I remember one time my dad had my brother, my sisters, and me sit down in the living room so he could wash our feet, apologize for his mistakes, and then tell us how he wanted to serve us.

I mean, think about that.

My dad. A pastor. Admitting his fault and apologizing to me as an adolescent. It's easy for people to think pastors believe they are never wrong. And if they ever are wrong, they find Scripture that somehow still proves they are right. Maybe some pastors do that but not my dad. Not my parents, thankfully. I was well-nurtured as a child in true, Spirit-filled principles that created a wonderful environment for us.

WHEN I WENT ALL IN

Do you remember your born again birthday? The day you gave your life to Jesus? Well, if you're like me, you don't. I gave my life to the Lord at some point in grade school, basically because I was able to grasp the concept of hell. I definitely didn't want to go there. So the sinner's prayer was a no-brainer for me. I just recited the prayer because heaven sounded way better than hell.

After that, I went through the awful atrocities of

the public school system as a teenager. Thousands of kids together with countless insecurities and problems was a nightmare for many of us. As I mentioned, I grew up around the popular crowd. Hanging out with this group wasn't the best when it came to helping me make godly decisions. I was influenced by people that weren't running after the Lord.

Up until this point in my life, I was complacent and lukewarm. Living in a way that would hopefully get me into heaven if I died, while still finding the fulfillment I desired in the world.

Then, something happened in my church. When I was 16 years old, my brother, Cyle, invited one of his friends to church. His name is Zach. Zach was a bona fide stud muffin. All the guys wanted to be him, and all the girls wanted to be with him. I was blown away that he was actually coming to our church! Little did I know, the Lord was doing a massive work in Zach's life. Through a series of different events, Bible studies, and people caring for him, Zach gave his life to Jesus. However, Zach didn't just say a prayer so he wouldn't go to hell. No, this was something different. He had a passion and fire for Jesus that I didn't have. That fire ignited something in my brother and then ignited a fire in me. I realized, with the help of my brother and Zach's example, what being a Christian was all about.

I realized it was about knowing Christ personally.

As I began walking with the Lord, he led me through many hills and valleys. I remember along the journey, the Holy Spirit led me to find a different group of friends at school.

For me, this was *extremely* difficult. I found so much of my identity in the group of people I was around. I had no friends outside of them. That is, friends that met my self-focused desires. Desires like having a high social status and to be liked by everyone. What was I going to do without these people? Was I going to have to sit by myself at lunch? For a teenager, those questions can be scary. I didn't want to be a loser. I was afraid,

but he led me through it.

After several months of inner friction with the Holy Spirit, I stepped out of the boat and onto the water. My water was trusting God that I could still be someone apart from the people I had identified with. They were wonderful people whom God loves dearly, but people who were having a greater influence on me than I was on them.

Eventually, I realized that knowing him was better than anything. And so it began. I was all in. I would have many other opportunities to pick up my cross and follow him as life went on, but this one significantly set the course for my life. One that would help me become more rooted and grounded in him.

I began to seek him daily in life. I began to discover the priceless riches of knowing him. I started reading my Bible every chance I could. I would spend hours alone with the Lord in worship and devotion. It was one of the sweetest seasons of my life.

However, as time went on, the honeymoon phase with the Holy Spirit seemed to disappear. I found it difficult to keep him a top priority in my life. I started struggling to have time with God, and that was one of the core principles I was taught growing up.

I would hear it from my parents. I would hear it from preachers on TV or on the car radio. I would go to church, and they'd be telling everyone the same thing. I'd hear it at conferences, summer trips, and every Wednesday night at youth group. My leaders would continually stress how important it was to have personal time with God. They'd say things like, "Don't expect the life you desire if time with him isn't a priority." "You have to make time with God important in your life." "If you are too busy for God, then you're too busy." "You *should* have time with God." "You *need* to have time with God." "You *have* to have time with God."

It's such great advice. It's absolutely true too. I am so thankful to have grown up in a church community and environment that emphasized the importance of spending time with God. Out of all the things I've been taught, this has been the most important. The greatest contributor to whatever success, significance, or fulfillment I have gained came from learning this lesson.

WHAT IS TIME WITH GOD?

For some of us, the concept of time with God may be a bit unfamiliar so let's briefly go over what time with God is. To this point, I've mainly used the phrase *time with God* as the way to describe intentional moments alone with God. There are many other terms that I'll be using in this book: *quiet time*, *the secret place*, and *alone time*. Others are *face-to-face time*, *the prayer closet*, *meditation*, and *hanging out with Jesus*. There are many more but they all convey the same idea: intentionally and individually seeking God. To help reduce confusion, the phrase we'll stick with mostly is *time with God*.

WHY DO WE NEED TO HAVE TIME WITH GOD?

From a Biblical approach, the answer to this question is that Jesus modeled it for us. Luke 5:16 (TPT) tells us, "Jesus

"Don't expect the life you desire if time with him isn't a priority."

"You have to make time with God important in your life."

"If you are too busy for God, then you're too busy."

"You *should* have time with God."

"You *need* to have time with God."

"You *have* to have time with God."

often slipped away from them and went into the wilderness to pray." It says that he would intentionally withdraw from the crowds and disciples to pray. Jesus also tells us in Matthew 6:5-6 (TPT), "But whenever you pray, go into your innermost chamber and be alone with Father God, praying to him in secret. And your Father, who sees all you do, will reward you openly."

The English Standard Version says it like this, "But when you pray, go into your room and shut the door and pray to your Father who is in secret. And your Father who sees in secret will reward you."

Jesus was likely instructing us both literally and metaphorically. It's good to physically be alone like Luke 5:16 depicts, but there are, of course, plenty of examples that the Lord gives us of praying in front of others. Ultimately, the Lord wants to get at the heart level with us. One of the best ways for that to happen is through one-on-one time with him. So why do we have time with God? Because Jesus did it and instructed us to do it also.

WHAT DOES TIME WITH GOD LOOK LIKE?

Generally speaking, it involves prayer and his Word. We pray to talk and hear him. We read the Bible to gain wisdom, insight, clarity, and to help gain a reliable understanding of his nature.

It doesn't have to consist only of these two parts, but they are usually standard components that help us connect with the Lord. There can be much more involved in our times with God like worship music, doing things we enjoy, etc.

THE PARABLE OF THE SOWER

One thing is for sure, the enemy of our souls doesn't want us having time with God. Time with him is the core place where we come alive. It's the place where we begin fulfilling the desires of God's heart. It's the starting place of where the enemy's plans are destroyed. Our time with God establishes in our minds our true identity as sons and daughters of him. The seed of his Word is planted in our hearts and the Garden of Eden is restored in our lives. The enemy doesn't want any of this.

The Parable of the Sower (Mark 4:1-20) shows us three reasons why God's Word doesn't develop in our lives. It can be reflective of a relationship with him that isn't growing.

1. *Satan appears and snatches the seed from our hearts.* He snatches the Word from us through lies. These lies prevent us from seeking God in the secret place.

2. *Our hearts fail to sink deep roots into the Word.* We don't endure in the secret place because of troubles or persecution. When life doesn't go as we had hoped, we try to find our quality of life somewhere other than a personal relationship with God through the Holy Spirit.

3. *The cares of this life choke out the Word of God.* The flashy things this world has to offer distract us. We are swayed away, not necessarily because of blatant lies, doubt, or troubles, but because we believe something is of greater worth than knowing Jesus.

These three occurrences prevent the Word of God from taking root in our lives. If we fall away from personal devotion with the Lord, then our lives will not grow as God desires for us. However, if we keep having consistent time with God in our lives, the Word of God will fall on good ground. The result will be a beautiful garden in our hearts and minds. One filled with heavenly thoughts and perspectives. The fruit of the Spirit will grow and the weeds will be uprooted.

MORE CHALLENGES

Another challenge I found myself facing was trying to keep sustained time with God through my own strength and determination. I've used literal timers to keep track of how much time I had spent with God. I've set alarms and notifications to go off. I've put time with God on my to do list. I've strategically placed Bibles throughout every area I would go in my day. One Bible next to my bed. One in the bathroom. One in the car. One on my office desk. I made sure the Bible app was front and center and at the easiest to access place on my phone's home screen. I tried it all.

None of those things are bad but what would eventually happen is the Bibles would start to collect dust. I would look at them and think to myself, "I should read the Word. Well, I really need to get going with my day. I'll read it later." Which many times wouldn't happen. Then, I'd start the soft shameful thoughts to make sure I knew that I should have done better for God. "Brice, you've got to do better tomorrow. It's been two days since you last read your Bible." Then, two days became three days and so on and so on. Have you ever had thoughts like that?

The days would turn into weeks so I'd crank up the internal shame a bit. "If you really loved God you'd make time with him a greater priority. You need to fast because your priorities are all messed up. Maybe you're just destined to be like the seed that gets choked out. You clearly care about other things more than God." I'd struggle with these types of thoughts. I would transfer my lack of effort and works into internal shame, guilt, and condemnation; I thought that's what I deserved. The lie of shame is a nasty thing.

My story went like this: I knew about God. Then, I came to know God personally. The relationship was awesome; however, after a while I started struggling to keep him first in my life. I tried and tried and then tried harder. I'd go through good seasons of keeping time with him a high priority, then I'd go through times that I didn't. I'd deal with thoughts of shame and continue on with what seemed like a never ending cycle of defeat.

However, all of that changed.

The Lord walked with me and taught me why I was struggling so much in keeping time with him a top priority. He gave insight to the various obstacles I couldn't seem to get over. He showed me how to overcome them. In the following chapters, I will share with you what the Lord shared with me.

REFLECTION

Spend some time reflecting on these questions. Use the space provided to journal and write down what the Holy Spirit is speaking to you.

1. Now that you know my background story regarding personal time with God, what's yours? Take some time to reflect on it.

2. What's your current personal time with God like (e.g., non-existent, hit or miss, pretty good, eager to learn more about this new adventure, etc.)?

3. If your personal time with God isn't where you'd like it to be, which example in the Parable of the Sower do you feel most identifies with you?

REFLECTION

Use the space provided below to write any personal revelations you've received. Write down words, phrases, or desires that are stirred within you. You can draw pictures that you may have seen in your mind while reading this chapter. This is a blank canvas to express your heart.

CHAPTER 2

HOW WE'RE WIRED

Nothing compares to the presence of God.

Words just seem to fall short in describing how wonderful the presence of the Lord is. The glory and majesty of his presence is so great it can even be terrifying! Look at some of these crazy encounters people had with God in the Bible.

- On Mount Sinai, Moses encountered the Lord with lightning and thunder. He left the interaction literally glowing.

- Elijah also encountered the Lord on Mount Sinai and experienced lightning, thunder, an earthquake, and a whisper.

- Jacob met an angel of the Lord who had the appearance of a man (Jesus) and insisted that he receive a blessing from him. He got what he wanted but in the process was left with a limp.

- Saul (turned Paul) ran into Jesus on the road to Damascus and was left blind for several days by the experience.

- Peter, James, and John got a special invite from Jesus to take a trip up the Mount of Transfiguration. During the hike, Jesus became dazzling white and shone like the sun. Moses and Elijah then appeared and started talking with the Lord. Peter was so frightened he offered to start building houses for them.

These are just a few accounts of what can happen when the Lord appears before men in his glory. There are many more but the point is clear - there is nothing like the presence of God. It's the place our hearts long to be, even if it leaves us terrified.

I remember one time being in a worship service and the presence of the Lord was moving so powerfully on me, I felt like my chest was going to burst. I had never experienced such extravagant love like that before. It was pure bliss. That experience, and others like it, left me knowing that the healing touch of God is stronger than the deepest hurt from Man. There's nothing the presence of God cannot do.

As we talk about time with God as it pertains to the presence of the Lord, it's necessary to mention the place in Scripture where God's presence was most often revealed. That is the temple described in the Old Testament. The temple was a place where God's people would come and draw near to him.

The presence of God was not restricted to the temple

for as David wrote in Psalm 139:7-12, we can never escape his presence. But the temple was generally the place for people to come and commune with God. To make sacrifices, worship, and to get right with him. It was a place that God met with his people.

It's important to have a clear understanding of the temple and its purpose because it helps us see how we can commune with the Lord now. Let's look at some different details of the temple of God.

THE TEMPLE LAYOUT

The temple was constructed into three separate areas: the Outer Court, the Holy Place, and the Holy of Holies. The Outer Court was the outermost area of the temple. Here, priests would perform sacrifices for the people as instructed by God to make atonement for their sins.

The next area, inside of the Outer Courts, was the Holy Place. This was a small, room-like chamber that certain priests would enter after sacrifices were made. It held different furnishings like the golden lamp stand, the table of his presence, and the golden altar of incense.

On the side opposite the entrance to the Holy Place was a veil, separating the Holy Place from the Holy of Holies. Only the high priest was allowed into the Holy of Holies.

Like the Holy Place, the Holy of Holies contained different objects as well. A key item is the Ark of the Covenant. It was a gold-covered wooden chest that held several items inside of it. On top of the box was the mercy seat. This represented God's throne and the place in which he dwelled.

That is a very brief overview of the temple and what was involved there. The most important thing for us to take from it is that the temple served as the place where God connected with his people. God wanted the temple constructed exactly as he instructed because he wanted us to have a clear picture of what Christ would do for us. Hebrews 8:1-5 (TPT) says,

> *Now this is the crowning point of what we are saying: We have a magnificent King-Priest who ministers for us at the right hand of God. He is enthroned with honor next to the throne of the Majesty on high. He serves in the holy sanctuary in the true heavenly tabernacle set up by God, and not by men.*
>
> *Since every high priest is appointed to offer both gifts and sacrifices, so the Messiah also had to bring some sacrifice. But since he didn't qualify to be an earthly priest, and there are already priests who offer sacrifices prescribed by the law, he offered in heaven a perfect sacrifice.*
>
> *The priests on earth serve in a temple that is but a copy modeled after the heavenly sanctuary; a shadow of the reality. For when Moses began to construct the tabernacle God warned him and said,*
>
> *'You must precisely follow the pattern I revealed to you on Mt. Sinai.'*

This passage tells us that the earthly tabernacle and temple were not the originals. They were copies of the true one in heaven. When Jesus came and died for us, there was clearly much more going on than what was in the natural. He himself was sacrificed at the altar of the Outer Courts, then ushered in to the Holy of Holies as our high priest, to sprinkle his blood on the mercy seat so that we could come before God the Father.

THE NEW COVENANT TEMPLE OF GOD

What does all this mean for us now? Now that Christ has done all this for us, how do we access the Holy of Holies? Let's start answering those questions by looking at 1 Corinthians 3:16 (NKJV) which says, "Do you not know that you are God's temple and that God's Spirit dwells in you?" Also Romans 8:11 (ESV) which says, "the Spirit of Him who raised Jesus from the dead dwells in you."

Both of these passages clearly state two things. 1) As believers in Christ, we are now the temples of God and 2) his Spirit lives in us. Remember, God wanted the Old Testament temple built carefully because it modeled the heavenly temple. There has always been the original, heavenly temple where God the Father resides, but there is also still an earthly temple. The New Covenant temple is Man. Jesus, being the firstborn of creation, kicked things off for us. Did he not call himself a temple in John 2:19?

There are parallels between the Old Testament temple and the New Testament temple that God wants us to see because it affects how we live in his presence today. I doubt God wanted Moses to build the temple carefully because he is an overbearing perfectionist. No, Jesus would come and be the earthly temple and believers after him would follow in his footsteps. The Father wanted Moses to be careful in following the layout instructions because it would model how we minister to God in the secret place today.

We can break down our human makeup into three main parts: spirit, soul, and body. I've included a diagram on page 32 of the Old Testament temple and the New Testament temple to help convey the parallels between the two. I had heard from a young age that we are made up of spirit, soul, and body.

The Old Covenant temple modeled how we minister to God in the secret place today.

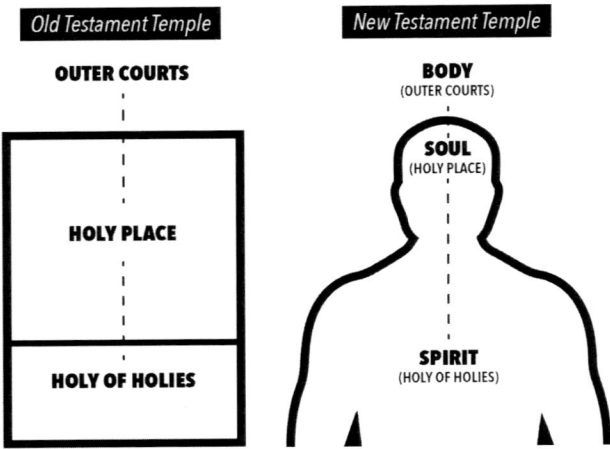

I went on to college at Oral Roberts University and their mission statement was "Educating every student - spirit, mind (soul), and body." However, I received all of this information as nothing more than, well, information. Eventually, the Lord showed me how important understanding this is so that we can live the way he intends.

Why? Think of it this way.

We're driving down the road and enjoying the wonderful scenery God has created. As we're driving we hear a loud "BANG" from under the hood. All of a sudden everything starts to shake. The car begins to sputter to a stop. We veer to the side of the road and what do we do next? We pop the hood, get out of the car, and see if we can figure out what's wrong with the vehicle.

Now, this is no mystery. We know that likely the problem is somewhere under the hood since that's where we heard the sound. It's easy to tell the problem isn't in the cab nor is it in the frame or exterior of the vehicle. The problem is at the core. It's in the engine bay.

Like vehicles, we are made up of different parts. In order for us to operate properly, we need to be able to identify where we are not functioning as God intends.

The Lord began to show me that there is a natural process of his presence as it pertains to how we are made. *This flow of his presence is crucial to keeping the secret place a top priority in our lives.* We are made up of separate parts and all of those parts are connected to one another. Like a vehicle's power comes from its engine - our power comes from our spirits.

> *God wants us to live first and foremost from our spirits.*

Our spirits are like our engines. They are what give us the power to move forward. Our souls (mind, will, and emotions) are like the cab of the vehicle - the place we are most familiar with and where we let those closest to us inside. Our bodies are like the exterior of the vehicle.

Up until the point of God revealing this to me, I realized that most of my times with God were happening at the soul level. My mind, will, and emotions were heavily engaged, but I wasn't fully engaged at the area where everything should have been starting from - my spirit.

I was focused on trying to make everything good inside the cab without turning the car on. It's like expecting the A/C to blow cold air without drawing power from the engine. It doesn't work that way. The air becomes cool when the engine is in use.

I wanted God to show up in the cab (my mind, will, and emotions), but I was neglecting the fact that his presence begins at my spirit - my Holy of Holies. This was causing problems in my life. I'd have times with God for seasons but eventually something would happen. I'd get stuck on the side of the road, scratching my head trying to figure out what the problem was.

Why didn't I really care to have time with God?
Why was I bored in the secret place?
How come I didn't have a desire to seek the Lord?
Was I not trying hard enough?

It's important for us to understand that we are now the temples of God and that God dwelled in the Holy of Holies. For us that means he dwells in our spirits. This is the foundational lesson that the Lord laid in me. From there, he continued to build upon it as I'll share in the coming chapters.

The presence of God
begins in our spirits.

REFLECTION

Spend some time reflecting on these questions. Use the space provided to journal and write down what the Holy Spirit is speaking to you.

1. Take a moment, close your eyes, and meditate on 1 Corinthians 3:16 (*"Do you not know that you are God's temple and that God's Spirit dwells in you?"*). What thoughts does the Holy Spirit bring to your mind?

2. What's your reaction to the truth that you are God's temple and like the temple you consist of three separate parts?

REFLECTION

Use the space provided below to write any personal revelations you've received. Write down words, phrases, or desires that are stirred within you. You can draw pictures that you may have seen in your mind while reading this chapter. This is a blank canvas to express your heart.

CHAPTER 3

SOUL-LED OR SPIRIT-LED

So, let's just ask the question that many of us wonder.

What is a spirit?

That was honestly a question I had for a long time, and I didn't really know the answer. It can be hard to get a good grasp of our spirits because we live in a natural realm. Are they glowing orbs inside our bodies? If we had special spiritual glasses could we see them inside of us? Our spirits aren't glowing orbs so let's take a look at some Scripture for help. John 4:24 (TPT) tells us, "God is Spirit..." Daniel 7:9 (NKJV) gives us a glimpse of his image. This verse says, "the Ancient of Days was seated; His garment was white as snow, and the hair of His head was like pure wool..."

These two verses show us that God is Spirit and that he has a form. He has an appearance that looks like we do. He can sit down. He has white clothing and a head with hair. From this, we can conclude that our spirits, since we are made in the image of God, look like him. Meaning our spirits aren't glowing orbs. We carry an appearance similar to what we see in the natural realm.

There's an amazing account given by a man named Dean Braxton on what heaven is like. Dean was clinically dead for nearly two hours and gives an incredible report of what happened during that time. What he shares is Biblically rooted and with everything he describes he includes this statement: it's all about Jesus. His testimony supports the claim that spiritual things aren't incomprehensible or indistinguishable. Our spirits have shape and form just like God does.

God is spirit and God was before creation. We have to accept the reality that things in the natural came from things of the spiritual. Spirit is where everything began and it's no different for us on an individual level.

But a big problem for us is that we are living from a soul or body first approach. This is easy to do because we can perceive both of these parts more naturally than the things of the spirit. We know our thoughts. We can easily engage with them. We know our will and the desires inside of us. We know what we feel in our emotions. We know what our physical bodies want. All that comes naturally for us. However, God wants us to be led by the Spirit, not by the flesh.

A major part of what I was learning was how to distinguish between being led by the Spirit and being led by my soul. It's important for us to learn the difference so the secret place remains a priority and, as a result, we can properly function in life. God wants our entire being powered by the Spirit. Galatians 5:16-17 (TPT) says,

> *As you yield freely and fully to the dynamic life and power of the Holy Spirit, you will abandon the cravings of your self-life. For your self-life craves the things that offend the Holy Spirit and hinder him from living free within you!*
>
> *And the Holy Spirit's intense cravings hinder your old self-life from dominating you! So then, the two incompatible and conflicting forces within you are your self-life of the flesh and the new creation life of the Spirit.*

Oh, that's so good. What I love is how the power of the Holy Spirit is so much stronger than our self-life when we yield to him. Here we see that there are two forces at work within us. It's important to realize that our sin nature happens in our soul and body. If we are born again in Jesus Christ, then our spirits are completely new. We are the righteousness of God through Christ Jesus.

Our spirits are completely renewed but our souls and bodies haven't yet reached salvation's completion. This doesn't mean our souls and bodies are bad. These are wonderful gifts from God, but they're not fit to lead our lives.

I remember for years I would read this verse and get down on myself because I'd see that I should be Spirit-led and not desire the things of the sin nature. However, I'd continually gratify the desires of the flesh. I didn't know what was wrong with me. Maybe I needed to read the Bible more. Maybe I wasn't actually even saved.

But what really was happening was I was living from the wrong part of me. I thought God and the core of me was at the soul level. I was looking for him in the wrong place.

His presence begins in the Holy of Holies within us (our spirits), not the Holy Place (our souls). He can certainly manifest and touch our lives at the soul or body level, and he does so often. However, it all begins at the spirit. I had the wrong approach. John 4:24 (TPT) says, "For God is a Spirit, and he longs to have sincere worshipers who worship and adore him in the realm of the Spirit and in truth."

He wants us to come to him on the paradigm of spirit, not soul or body! This is challenging because we feel validated by our feelings. We are born in a world that tells us what we feel is real. If we feel it then we have some basis to believe what's happening inside us is truly happening.

Our spirits don't operate like our souls do. Our spirits are always and continually desiring to search out the truths of God and his nature. We're seated with him in heavenly places so they should! In Christ, that's how we are. Our identity is in him. We have to stop trying to validate truth through the filter of our mind, will, and emotions. They're just not designed or equipped to process Kingdom realities!

But our spirits are.

I love the feelings I get in the presence of God. I love to be elated by his love and acceptance. And in no way is it wrong to experience these things. They're good. However, they're just not designed to sustain a strong connection between God and us. When we learn how to worship him in spirit and truth, we begin to let our engines power our lives. Our souls aren't equipped to power our desire to seek God in the secret place.

That doesn't mean we won't have struggles or bad days. However, the struggles and bad days will become less and less because we let the source of life lead the way. Remember that in the garden, Adam did not become a living

The Father is seeking people who worship him in spirit and truth - not soul and truth or body and truth.

being until God breathed his Spirit into him.

Genesis 2:7 (NKJV) says, "then the Lord God formed man of the dust of the ground and breathed into his nostrils the breath of life, and the man became a living being."

Adam was a physical creation before he was alive. When God, who is Spirit, breathed into him, he then became alive. It's so important for us to really see that we are spiritual beings at our core. Our souls and bodies are part of us but not the core of us.

SO HOW DO WE LIVE FROM OUR SPIRITS?

Learning how to live from our spirits rather than our souls or bodies can seem confusing. Again, we can feel what's happening in our souls. We can feel what's happening in our bodies. But how do we live from the place of our spirits? Let me share with you what I felt the Lord explain to me.

During one of my times with the Lord, I was bored. This was during a pretty long "drought" season of my life. I was seeking the Lord but it wasn't exciting. It wasn't enthralling. There was no resemblance to the deep romance we read about in Song of Songs.

I was there to punch my time card. I had been taught and told that I needed to have time with God, so to feel good about myself I was doing that. I had my Bible out with some worship music on. My phone kept sounding off alarms and notifications so I figured I'd better put it on silent because it was distracting me from reading the Bible.

And as I began to read the text again I just asked the Lord, "Why is it like this? Why don't I care like I used to? I'd much rather be working on the things I need to get done today. I'd much rather be checking out football articles. I'm bored in your presence. I know that it's something wrong on my end, but I just can't figure it out, Lord."

He began to show me that when I went all in with him in high school, I realized that the Bible is filled with amazing truths and revelation. I came to discover that the Bible has hidden gems throughout the text. And these hidden gems of knowledge and understanding are life changing.

For years I would go into my time with the Lord by turning the worship music on and opening my Bible up. Then, I'd start digging for the hidden gems of wisdom and understanding. I wanted to know more. I wasn't necessarily doing it for selfish reasons or to try and wow people with some advanced knowledge I had gained. I genuinely loved the experience of having my mind opened to the truths of heaven. It was wonderful. However, what was happening in those experiences was happening primarily at the soul level. My mind was processing the information and my emotions were getting a thrill from it.

My mind, will, and emotions were leading my time with the Lord but my spirit was in idle.

After over a decade of doing this, the gems of knowledge became harder and harder to find. I'd go and seek out other preachers to try and get their different perspectives on passages in the Bible. My heart-to-heart connection with God had become dependent on whether I was learning something new or not. The problem with knowledge is that it will eventually cease. 1 Corinthians 13:8-12 (ESV) tells us this:

> *Love never ends. As for prophecies, they will pass away; as for tongues, they will cease; as for knowledge, it will pass away. For we know in part and we prophesy in part, but when the perfect comes, the partial will pass away. When I was a*

child, I spoke like a child, I thought like a child, I reasoned like a child. When I became a man, I gave up childish ways. For now we see in a mirror dimly, but then face to face. Now I know in part; then I shall know fully, even as I have been fully known.

What the Lord was showing me was that my time with him was not happening in a sustainable way. I was seeking him with the wrong motive. Don't get me wrong, I knew what worshiping in spirit and truth was, and I was doing it at some level. Primarily, though, my motive was to gain wisdom and get an emotional rush from it - not to commune with him.

And that's where the big revelation hit me. God wasn't calling me to time with him just to become filled with more knowledge. He was calling me to come and feast with him. Many times throughout the Bible we see the Lord painting a picture of us coming to a table and feasting with him.

You prepare a table before me in the presence of my enemies. (Psalm 23:5, ESV)

Everyone who thirsts, come to the waters; And you who have no money, come, buy and eat. Yes, come, buy wine and milk without money and without price. Why do you spend money for what is not bread, And your wages for what does not satisfy?

Listen carefully to Me, and eat what is good, and let your soul delight itself in abundance. Incline your ear, and come to Me. Hear, and your soul shall live; And I will make an everlasting covenant with you. (Isaiah 55:1-4, NKJV)

Now as they were eating, Jesus took bread, and after blessing it broke it and gave it to the disciples, and said, 'Take, eat;

this is my body.' And he took a cup, and when he had given thanks he gave it to them, saying, 'Drink of it, all of you,' (Matthew 26:26-27, ESV)

Write this: Blessed are those who are invited to the marriage supper of the Lamb. (Revelation 19:9, ESV)

God loves to eat! No, not physical food - he is Spirit. He loves for us to come and eat of the bread and drink of the wine that is him. It's wonderful to learn from him but that's not the primary motive of time with God. Gaining knowledge isn't the ultimate goal of fellowship with Jesus. The point is simply God-to-Man, heart level connection.

It's about friendship. It's about walking with him just like Adam and Eve did in the beginning. We have restored relationship with our Creator. He wants us to walk in the garden, enjoying the feast of the fruit of his Spirit that he offers. Love, joy, peace, patience, kindness, goodness, gentleness, faithfulness, and self-control.

He invites us to come and feast on his nature.

After he showed me this, a verse came to my mind in John 7:38 (ESV) that says, "Whoever believes in me, as the Scripture has said, 'Out of his heart will flow rivers of living water.'" Several translations use the word "belly" rather than heart here, and that was the word I have been most familiarized with at this point.

I felt the Lord showing me that our spirits are like bellies, like stomachs. I've always thought that was a peculiar way to put it. Why would he say our spirits are comparable to bellies? What I felt him showing me was that the purpose of a stomach is to take food and supply life to the rest of the body. Bellies don't care how many times they've had the same meal. Our spirits are like bellies - they couldn't care less how many times they've feasted on the same truths of God!

They just want to feast on the truths of God and supply life to our souls and physical bodies.

Our minds are like our mouths. Mouths love to taste food. Our minds love to taste knowledge. However, like mouths tend to get bored with the same food over time, so our minds get bored with the same knowledge over time.

Our minds love to learn new things. We get excited from fresh knowledge. It gives us a different outlook and a bit of a rush. Eventually, it becomes harder and harder to learn something new. We have to spend more time than we used to trying to learn new things. So it becomes more difficult in our times with God to find the same sense of purpose and fulfillment that we once had. We eventually may read the whole Bible. We hear most of the theological perspectives. We become accustomed to coming before him with the wrong approach. And then we start to get bored. But we know that God is not boring!

Don't get me wrong. I'm not saying that wisdom is of no value. Gaining understanding is so important. Proverbs 4:7 (ESV) says, "The beginning of wisdom is this: Get wisdom, and whatever you get, get insight."

We should absolutely desire wisdom and understanding; however, this is not the foundation on which we build our friendship with God. Gaining knowledge should come from a place of seeking the Lord on a heart-to-heart level. It happens as a natural result of feasting with the Lord in a love relationship. Our relationship with the Lord shouldn't be predicated on whether or not we are gaining knowledge or getting an emotional high.

For example, let's take the truth that God loves us. If I take that truth and treat it as knowledge for my mind to learn, eventually it loses its luster. My mind says, "Yeah okay, I've already learned that. Teach me something new." However, if I treat that truth as eternal food that my entire being needs to eat each day in order to truly live, then it takes on a whole different meaning. That truth becomes my source of life. We never graduate from the truth that God loves us. We don't just check it off the list of things we've learned about God. Yes, I learn it with my mind but my spirit desires to feast on that truth every day forever and ever.

THE RIVER OF LIFE

Here's another interesting thought to consider as we learn how to live from our spirits. Revelation 22:1-2 (TPT) says,

> *Then the angel showed me the river of the water of life, flowing with water clear as crystal, continuously pouring out from the throne of God and of the Lamb. The river was flowing in the middle of the street of the city, and on either side of the river was the Tree of Life, with its twelve kinds of ripe fruit according to each month of the year.*

Visualize this river. We read that it begins at the throne of the Lamb of God. From there it flows through the middle of the street of the city. The text doesn't explicitly state where the river goes next. Does the river of life flow to the edge of nothingness - kind of like Asgard in the movie Thor? I've got a feeling the answer to that is, no. Rivers always have outlets; otherwise they become stagnant and dead, just like the Dead Sea.

Jesus does tell us in John 7:38 that anyone who

believes in him will have "rivers of living water" flow out of their inner-most being. What if you and I are the next destination point for the river of life? What if the river goes from his throne, through the city, and then to our hearts like Jesus mentions? Scripture clearly reveals that there is a connection between the heart of heaven and the heart of Man. Check out this verse in Psalm 46:4 (TPT). It says, "God has a constantly flowing river whose sparkling streams bring joy and delight to his people. His river flows right through the city of God Most High, in his holy dwelling places."

Did you catch it? Jesus wasn't kidding or just saying something that sounds nice. There is a very real river of life that's filled with joy and delight to satisfy God's people. It's not something to experience only after our bodies die. It's something for the here and now. We are his holy dwelling places and his Word says that the river flows right through the city of God Most High, into his holy dwelling places.

"Places" is plural - meaning there is more than one dwelling place. That's you and me, beloved. Let your heart and mind run wild in this truth! The fullness of joy and unlimited pleasures (Psalm 16:11) that are found in his presence are flowing within us. God made the way we activate the flow of the river of life from our spirits very simple: just believe. Simply believe in him and that his life is flowing in you.

Don't wait for your feelings to validate it. Just simply believe. God wants to satisfy all of humanity with his love, joy, and delight and he has done everything to make it available to us right now. He's not holding back. He wants to lift us up to places of joyful bliss that we've never experienced before. *We just have to stop waiting to feel it first in our bodies and souls because that's not where he's promised it will start from!*

We simply need to believe it is ours; to believe that it is already in us and is our inheritance through Christ Jesus! It's ours for the taking. It's his great pleasure to give us the Kingdom (Luke 12:32), and his Kingdom is full of joy and pleasures that last forever! I love Paul's prayer in Ephesians. See how Paul expresses the river of life that is ready to flow from God through us in Ephesians 3:16-19 (TPT).

> *And I pray that he would unveil within you the unlimited riches of his glory and favor until supernatural strength floods your innermost being with his divine might and explosive power. Then, by constantly using your faith, the life of Christ will be released deep inside you, and the resting place of his love will become the very source and root of your life.*
>
> *Then you will be empowered to discover what every holy one experiences—the great magnitude of the astonishing love of Christ in all its dimensions. How deeply intimate and far-reaching is his love! How enduring and inclusive it is! Endless love beyond measurement that transcends our understanding—this extravagant love pours into you until you are filled to overflowing with the fullness of God!*

We just have to stop waiting to feel it first in our bodies and souls because that's not where he's promised it will start from!

REFLECTION

Spend some time reflecting on these questions. Use the space provided to journal and write down what the Holy Spirit is speaking to you.

1. I routinely had time with God for the thrill of revelation knowledge or to fulfill a religious obligation. In what ways do you feel you have incorrectly approached nearness with God?

2. After reading about the river of life, what does it look like to you? How do you see it flowing in and through you?

REFLECTION

Use the space provided below to write any personal revelations you've received. Write down words, phrases, or desires that are stirred within you. You can draw pictures that you may have seen in your mind while reading this chapter. This is a blank canvas to express your heart.

CHAPTER 4

GAZE UPON THE SON OF MAN

Get ready.

What I'm going to share with you in this chapter has dramatically changed my life. I pray it helps you as much as it's helped me. It has changed the way I approach God entirely. I used to lack confidence when I approached him. I had common issues of shame and guilt from sin but on top of that I was dealing with the struggles of figuring out if what was happening was really, well... even happening.

Was what was happening to me in my times with him from him, or were they things in my own imagination? I had heard different people talk about how the enemy can sneak into our thoughts and lead us astray. Yikes, I certainly didn't want that to happen. Oftentimes, I'd resort to the safe thing to do. I'd be cautious in seeking him. I figured it was better to be safe than deceived.

However, living safe just never seemed to cut it. There was something missing. The amazing stories and people I would read about in the Bible just weren't matching my life. I wasn't after an experience just so I could say I had an experience. I knew that my approach to God must have been missing something.

One day, I was going through my normal routine of time with God, and I came to the story of Philip and Nathanael. As I read the story, which I had read before, there was something different. The words were more alive than they ever were in the past. Here is what I read in John 1:43-51 (TPT).

The next day Jesus decided to go to the region of Galilee. There he found Philip and said to him, 'Come and follow me.' (Now Philip, Andrew, and Peter were all from the same village of Bethsaida.) Then Philip went to look for his friend, Nathanael, and told him, 'We've found him! We've found the One we've been waiting for! It's Jesus, son of Joseph from Nazareth, the Anointed One! He's the One that Moses and the prophets prophesied would come!' Nathanael sneered, 'Nazareth! What good thing could ever come from Nazareth?' Philip answered, 'Come and let's find out!'

When Jesus saw Nathanael approaching, he said, 'Now here comes a true son of Israel—an honest man with no hidden motive!' Nathanael was stunned and said, 'But you've never met me—how do you know anything about me?' Jesus answered, 'Nathanael, right before Philip came to you I saw you sitting under the shade of a fig tree.' Nathanael blurted out, 'Teacher, you are truly the Son of God and the King of Israel!'

It's amazing what's happened so far to Nathanael in this story. How quickly he goes from skeptic and doubter to boldly proclaiming, "Teacher, you are truly the Son of God and the King of Israel!" But what's so peculiar is the exchange between Jesus and Nathanael. I mean, why does Nathanael all of a sudden blurt out that he's convinced Jesus is the Son of God? All Jesus told him was that he saw him sitting under the shade of a fig tree. What's the big deal? Clearly, there's something more going on in the story than what we read.

I'd like to propose that while Nathanael was under the shade of the fig tree, he was having an encounter with the Holy Spirit. Perhaps he felt the Lord whispering to him that he was an honest man with no hidden motive. When Jesus and Nathanael meet, Jesus tells him the same thing he heard while alone in the Spirit. Curious and intrigued Nathanael says, "You don't even know me." To which Jesus responds (paraphrased), "Oh yes I do. I saw you under the fig tree. I was the one speaking to you." This is why Nathanael responds the way he did. What a powerful glimpse into the nearness of God in our lives. He truly is with us at all times. Now let's look at the rest of the passage.

> *Jesus answered, 'Do you believe simply because I told you I saw you sitting under a fig tree? You will experience even more impressive things than that! I prophesy to you eternal truth: <u>From now on you will see an open heaven and gaze upon the Son of Man</u> like a stairway reaching into the sky with the messengers of God climbing up and down upon him!'*

He tells him that from that point on he will see an open heaven and gaze upon the Son of Man! I want to know how Nathanael responded to such a promise. What was the look on his face like? He just gained revelation that Jesus is the

Son of God, and then Jesus tells him he will continually gaze upon him in a supernatural way.

Wow.

As I read that I groaned inside and said to myself, "I want what Nathanael was having!" And that's exactly what I began to ask of the Lord. I told him I wanted to gaze upon him like Nathanael did. We know that Jesus wasn't talking about something that would happen to Nathanael after he (Nathanael) died because Jesus told him it would be from that point on. Meaning, Nathanael would start experiencing the prophetic word in his life at that moment.

Why does God's promise to Nathanael matter to us? Because Nathanael's experience can be ours too. Jesus tells us if we ask him for something he will give it to us (specifically referring to the Holy Spirit).

> *Ask, and it will be given to you; seek, and you will find; knock, and it will be opened to you. For everyone who asks receives, and the one who seeks finds, and to the one who knocks it will be opened. (Matthew 7:7-8, ESV)*

Jesus promises us this. If we simply ask, then he will give us what we ask for. I began to seek this out more. Many times I had thoughts and ideas of Jesus, but like I mentioned before, I wasn't sure how much of it was just my imagination and how much was divinely inspired. That's what I wanted to know.

What was this "gazing upon the Son of Man" all about?

THE MOUNT OF TRANSFIGURATION

In chapter two, I mentioned some different examples of God manifesting his presence to people and what those experiences entailed. In that list, I mentioned Moses and Elijah's encounter with the Lord on Mount Sinai. I also included the three disciples' encounter with Jesus on the Mount of Transfiguration. It wasn't long after I asked the Lord to see him like Nathanael did that he revealed to me the powerful connection between these three encounters.

Let's first go through what happened at the Mount of Transfiguration in Matthew 17:1-8 (TPT). I highly encourage you to become enveloped by this story. Don't read through it quickly. Let their encounter become yours too.

Six days later Jesus took Peter and the two brothers, Jacob and John, and hiked up a high mountain to be alone. Then Jesus' appearance was dramatically altered. A radiant light as bright as the sun poured from his face. And his clothing became luminescent—dazzling like lightning. He was transfigured <u>before their very eyes</u>.

Then suddenly, Moses and Elijah appeared, and they spoke with Jesus. Peter blurted out, 'Lord, it's so wonderful that we are all here together! If you want, I'll construct three shrines, one for you, one for Moses, and one for Elijah.' But while Peter was still speaking, a radiant cloud composed of light spread over them, enveloping them all. And God's voice suddenly spoke from the cloud, saying, 'This is my dearly loved Son, the constant focus of my delight. Listen to him!'

The three disciples were dazed and terrified by this phenomenon, and they fell facedown to the ground. But Jesus walked over and touched them, saying, 'Get up and stop being afraid.' When they finally opened their eyes and looked around, they saw no one else there but Jesus.

What an encounter! Jesus became radiant with light as bright as the sun, and the disciples were dazed and terrified. It says that he was transfigured "before their very eyes." That's going to be a big deal for us as we explore these encounters. It's also important to point out that it was Moses and Elijah who appeared to Jesus and started talking to him.

Was it just coincidence that these were the two people who showed up on the scene? There were so many other people of great faith in the Bible. How come it wasn't Abraham and Noah? Why not David and Daniel or Joshua and Samuel? Surely there is a specific reason that it was Moses and Elijah who showed up on that mountain.

The relation is that both Moses and Elijah encountered God on a mountain like the disciples did. However, there is one key difference between Moses' and Elijah's experiences and the disciples' experience. Here are the two accounts of Moses and Elijah.

MOSES ON MOUNT SINAI

And the Lord said, 'I will cause all my goodness to pass in front of you, and I will proclaim my name, the Lord, in your presence. I will have mercy on whom I will have mercy, and I will have compassion on whom I will have compassion.' But, he said, 'you cannot see my face, for no one may see me and live.' Then the Lord said, 'There is a place near me where you may stand on a rock. When my glory passes by, I will put you in a cleft in the rock and cover you with my hand until I have passed by. Then I will remove my hand and you will see my back; but my face must not be seen.' (Exodus 33:19-23, NIV)

ELIJAH ON MOUNT SINAI

Then (The Lord) said (to Elijah), 'Go out, and stand on the mountain before the Lord.' And behold, the Lord passed by, and a great and strong wind tore into the mountains and broke the rocks in pieces before the Lord, but the Lord was not in the wind; and after the wind an earthquake, but the Lord was not in the earthquake; and after the earthquake a fire, but the Lord was not in the fire; and after the fire a still small voice. (1 Kings 19:11-12, NKJV)

Let's compare some things from these two encounters. We see specifically that the Lord "passed by" both Moses and Elijah. We know for sure that the Lord himself was present.

We also know that the Lord spoke to both Moses and Elijah. One interesting point is that in Exodus 33:11, the Bible says that Moses spoke with the Lord face-to-face, like friends talk to one another. This is peculiar because just a few verses later, the Lord tells Moses that he can't see his face, because if he does, he will die.

So which is it? Was Moses literally face-to-face with God or not? Verse 11 is likely using a type of speech. Moses spoke with the Lord like they were face-to-face but not meaning that Moses saw the face of God.

The point is that Moses' encounter was a very deep and powerful one, but he didn't see God's face. Elijah hears the voice of the Lord, but like Moses, he doesn't actually see his face. Two people that were called up a mountain to meet with the Lord, and two men that did not see his face. But what does the Bible clearly state about the three disciples' experience with Jesus?

The disciples saw Jesus' face.

That's a big deal. They saw the face of God in all his radiant light and glory. They saw it right there along with Moses and Elijah. This signified to us that we can now look at the face of God. We can look upon the face of God through his perfect Son, Jesus Christ.

This is a really, really, really big deal.

Because of the indwelling presence of Jesus through the Holy Spirit in us, we can now look upon the face of God! He doesn't have his back toward us like he did to Moses! Under the New Covenant in Christ, he is postured toward us. His face is completely exposed and his heart is fully open to us. He's inviting us into breathtaking friendship and harmonious communion.

We have access to gazing upon his glorious smile over us. Any anger or wrath that was ours has been placed on Jesus through the cross. The kind, non-verbal gestures that Jesus gets from the Father, we get too! Sure, we can disappoint the Lord and sadden his heart through disobedience. But because of Jesus we always have his smile. We always have his acceptance. There is no need to have any fear of separation. We don't ever have to wonder if God will walk out on us because of our failings or shortcomings. Christ is in us, and he will never leave us or forsake us.

The promise from the Lord made in Isaiah 54:9 (NLT) is now in effect just as the prophet declared it would be once Jesus died and rose for us! This verse says, "Just as I swore in the time of Noah that I would never again let a flood cover the earth, so now I swear that I will never again be angry and punish you."

We can see the fire in his eyes as he burns with passionate love. Those beautiful eyes that help us see into his heart and mind. They let us know how he feels about us.

They tell us that he has good plans for us.

Plans of hope and to prosper us. Plans of a good future. We see in his eyes the countless thoughts that he has toward us. They are good and so many that they outnumber the grains of sand on the entire earth!

Some may say, "Ok, so what? Jesus is not here in the flesh so there's no way to see his real face." But that's just not true! We are to walk by the Spirit. He resides in us now. Jesus said the Father would send the Holy Spirit who is exactly like him. So now through the Holy Spirit, Jesus dwells in us. He dwells where our faith in him is, and we are to walk by faith - not by our natural sight. Even though we only see in part, we shouldn't make little of its significance!

Remember, we are the temple of God, and he dwells in the Holy of Holies - the deepest part of us. That's where everything should start. Colossians 3:1 (NLT) says, "Since you have been raised to new life with Christ, set your sights on the realities of heaven, where Christ sits in the place of honor at God's right hand."

God is charging us to see him through the eyes of our hearts and imaginations. He extends an invitation to enjoy blissful friendship with him at the heart level. The way we can perceive it is on the canvas of our thoughts and imaginations!

The Holy Spirit resides at home in our spirit but he certainly isn't limited there. The Holy Place of the temple contained the table of his presence. It represents that we can experience fellowship and communion with him at our soul level: our mind, will, and emotions. The veil was ripped open signifying that we have full access into the heart of God and that he has access to come toward us too! I promise you, seeing the face of Jesus in faith at the place of our imaginations is a very divine thing. It isn't something we should consider to be just another one of our thoughts.

When we use our imaginations to see the face of God through faith, something supernatural happens.

Gazing upon Jesus helps us take delight in him and allows us to believe that he delights in us. This makes the secret place irresistible. His delight keeps us coming back for more. We are experiencing an aspect of relationship that God desires for us to have and enjoy every single day. And he wants us to have the encounter any time and as many times as we want! Acts 2:17 (NLT) says, "'In the last days,' God says, 'I will pour out my Spirit upon all people. Your sons and daughters will prophesy. *Your young men will see visions, and your old men will dream dreams.*'"

This verse is telling us that it's time for us to embrace our ability to see in the Spirit. We have his Word to give us insight regarding who he is and how he feels toward us. Now, the Spirit has been poured out and dwells inside of us!

We need to not put limits on this. We shouldn't wait around for God to zap us with a vision or a dream. The Holy Spirit has already been poured out and deposited in our hearts. Ask for the Holy Spirit to help you see him and he guarantees that he will answer us. In Luke 11:13 (NIV) he says, "how much more will your father in heaven give the Holy Spirit to those who ask?"

Don't be afraid to come before him boldly with this request. Don't say things like, "*If it's your will* then give me a vision, God." While sincere, those kinds of prayers are often dripping with doubt and unbelief. They provide a safety net in case nothing happens and place the blame on God if our expectations aren't met. His Word tells us that it *is* his will to give us the Holy Spirit and all the good gifts that come with him!

Just have confident trust that when you fix your mind on heavenly things, especially the face of Jesus, the Holy Spirit is at work in it. He is guiding your thoughts in truth and letting you have divine visions of him and his Kingdom. As simple as it is to do, thinking about Jesus and heavenly realities is a divine experience!

WE ARE CURRENTLY THERE

Not convinced? Still think seeing Jesus' face is only for the afterlife? It sounds wild to say but Scripture says we are actually already there. Heaven, that is Jesus, has been deposited in our hearts through the Holy Spirit. There's really no getting around it. The core of us, our spirits, are with him who *is* heaven. Hebrews 12:22-24 (TPT) says,

> By contrast, <u>we have already come near to God</u> in a totally different realm, the Zion-realm, for we have entered the city of the Living God, which is the New Jerusalem in heaven! <u>We have joined</u> the festal gathering of myriads of angels in their joyous celebration! And as members of the church of the Firstborn all our names have been legally registered as citizens of heaven! And <u>we have come before God</u> who judges all, and who lives among the spirits of the righteous who have been made perfect in his eyes! And <u>we have come to Jesus</u> who established a new covenant with his blood sprinkled upon the mercy seat; blood that continues to speak from heaven, 'forgiveness,' a better message than Abel's blood that cries from the earth, 'justice.'

And furthermore Ephesians 2:6 (TPT) says, "*He raised us up with Christ* the exalted One, and *we ascended with him* into the

Thinking about Jesus and heavenly realities is a divine experience!

glorious perfection and authority of the heavenly realm, for *we are now co-seated as one with Christ!*"

Those passages make it as clear as day for us! The Kingdom of heaven is already here. Didn't Jesus tell us this? Luke 17:20-22 (TPT) says,

> *Jesus was once asked by the Jewish religious leaders, 'When will God's kingdom realm come?' Jesus responded, 'God's kingdom realm does not come simply by obeying principles or by waiting for signs. The kingdom is not discovered in one place or another, for God's kingdom realm is already expanding within some of you.'*

We are already there. The Kingdom of heaven is in our midst and is expanding inside of us. There's no need to wait to see the face of Jesus and his glorious Kingdom. While seeing him in our minds may only be in part, it still has massive power to transform us!

THE EYE IS A LAMP

Let's look at another example of how "seeing" correlates to our inner being experiencing change. Matthew 6:22-23 (ESV) says,

> *The eye is the lamp of the body. So, if your eye is healthy, your whole body will be full of light, but if your eye is bad, your whole body will be full of darkness. If then the light in you is darkness, how great is the darkness!*

In the context of this verse, Jesus is telling us to store up treasures in heaven and to refrain from storing up earthly treasures. It seems a bit peculiar for him to tell us not to love material possessions and then go to talking about the eye and being filled with light or darkness. What can material possessions, our eyes, and being filled with light or darkness all have in common?

The way we store up treasures on earth is by first gaining a desire for it. It begins with envy, misplaced trust, lust, etc. Our physical eyes see the pleasures of the world and we become fascinated by them. After becoming fascinated by them, we pursue them.

On the contrary, if we want to store up treasures in heaven, it also begins with the eye. Not so much our physical eyes but the eyes of our understanding. It's our imaginations and thoughts. It's interesting because our physical eyes' purpose is to send our minds signals formed by natural light. It's there that we perceive what we are seeing.

Our minds are the actual place where we are seeing.

Close your eyes and imagine the Eiffel Tower. How is it that we can see things with our eyes closed? It's because our minds are where we are perceiving what we see. Jesus is telling us to see with our inner eyes the light of his Kingdom realities. The way we store up treasures in heaven is by first seeing into the heavenly realm. 1 John 1:5 (NIV) says, "God is light; in him there is no darkness at all."

God is light, and the way we get filled with the light is through seeing him! Our minds can get filled with two different sources of light - either the light that comes from desiring the world or the light that comes from desiring him. If we try and use the light that comes from the world to fill the desires of our hearts, we will soon discover the "light" was only darkness. However, when we look upon God, we will be filled with true light.

He wants us to see him and
the light that comes from him.

Our minds get renewed, our emotions get restored, and our wills get properly aligned. From that experience, we will be changed and overflowing with the light of God.

He wants us to use our physical eyes for his glory, but he doesn't want them to mislead us. He doesn't want them to lead us astray from seeing him, the Treasure of all treasures! The Treasure that will never fade away. I love how The Passion Translation says Matthew 6:22-23:

> *The eyes of your spirit allow revelation-light to enter into your being. If your heart is unclouded, the light floods in! But if your eyes are focused on money, the light cannot penetrate and darkness takes its place. How profound will be the darkness within you if the light of truth cannot enter!*

Gazing upon Jesus is a key part of how God wired us to live. It's essential if we want time with God to be a continual habit in our lives. Seeing the light from him helps us find our satisfaction and treasure in him. It's a core delight of our lives that keeps us coming back for more! The power of gazing upon Jesus with our imaginations has been severely underestimated by the Church. We have not taken full advantage of this opportunity he has given us. It's time for that to change!

God is light, and the way
we get filled with the light
is through seeing him!

REFLECTION

Spend some time reflecting on these questions. Use the space provided to journal and write down what the Holy Spirit is speaking to you.

1. As a believer, you are currently seated with Christ in heavenly places. Close your eyes and visualize this Kingdom reality. What do you see?

2. Hebrews 12:18-24 says we have already come to the city of God. Through the lens of this truth, imagine the environment. What do you see?

3. Our inner eye is a lamp to our being. If it sees the light of God, then it will begin to see the real treasures that come from knowing Christ. Close your eyes and see Jesus' loving expressions as he looks at you. What truths and/or feelings are you experiencing?

REFLECTION

Use the space provided below to write any personal revelations you've received. Write down words, phrases, or desires that are stirred within you. You can draw pictures that you may have seen in your mind while reading this chapter. This is a blank canvas to express your heart.

CHAPTER 5

HOW WE GAZE UPON HIM

Let's dive deeper.

When we are thinking about these higher realities, it's important to remember that it's not so much about the physical form of what we are seeing. Does Jesus have dark or light hair? What about his eye shape or his facial hair? These questions aren't the point of it all. Even those who aren't saved could gaze upon Jesus if that's all it was about.

We are looking to behold the truths of God more than his physical attributes.

For instance, I know that God smiles at me. I have his smile because of what Jesus did for us on the cross. Do I know exactly what his smile looks like? Probably not. But that isn't the point. The point is that I know I have his smile. I know that he takes great delight in me. I'm safe to come before him. There's no need to wallow in shame, condemnation, or guilt because I know how he feels about me. I can see it expressed through his smile.

Since I know that God takes great delight in me, I know that means he smiles at me. And since I can see him smiling at me, I know that he takes great delight in me. And it just keeps going back and forth. This unending cycle of truth-filled sustenance that feeds my inner being. It's a feast that creates a sustainable purpose to coming to him regularly in prayer. Our motivation behind time with God is no longer about gaining knowledge or fulfilling a religious obligation.

Gazing upon him in this way doesn't mean he approves of our disobedience. It simply means that his love is unwavering and secure, never failing or tapering off in response to our mistakes. Seeing his smile, his true nature toward those who are in Christ, doesn't give us permission to sin. It gives us the ability to overcome it.

It's like a bug that can't get its eyes off of the light. His smile draws us in closer and closer. His love brings us near as we gaze upon him. And it's there that the desire and lust for other things dies.

The primary way I have overcome sinful addictions and habits in my life is by fixing my eyes on him. Gazing into the passionate fire of love in his eyes. His love and fellowship are so much better than the best sin has to offer. We hear that said a lot in Christian circles, but we do very little to help people actually experience the bliss of communion with Jesus. Gaze upon him!

Literally think about and visualize him. Think about

him dancing and shouting proclamations over you like Zephaniah 3:17 tells us he does. See his mouth move and project the words of Isaiah 62:4 (NLT) to you,

> *Never again will you be called 'The Forsaken City' or 'The Desolate Land.' Your new name will be 'The City of God's Delight' and 'The Bride of God,' for the LORD delights in you and will claim you as his bride.*

Some may ask, "Does imagining Jesus really break the power of sin in my life?" The power of sin has already been broken through Jesus' death, burial, and resurrection. Imagining Jesus helps our souls get in correct alignment with heaven. A clear picture of truth helps us get to a place of believing, and believing is what causes the river of life to start overflowing from within us. Look at what Jesus said in John 5:19 (ESV). "Truly, truly, I say to you, the Son can do nothing of his own accord, but only what he sees the Father doing. For whatever the Father does, that the Son does likewise."

Jesus tells us his way of living life in the Father's will! Jesus only does what he sees the Father doing. Isn't that the way we do things in the natural too? As a child, I just watched my parents to learn how to do things. Whatever they did I would do. Even if they said one thing and did another, I would do what I saw them do.

Jesus was no different. He simply gazed upon the Father. Did Jesus have a special ability to see in the Spirit that we don't have? Nothing in the Bible suggests that. Jesus still had to learn and gain understanding. He wasn't born with it. Luke 2:52 (NIV) says, "And Jesus grew in wisdom and stature, and in favor with God and man."

So the wisdom of God, which is Christ (1 Corinthians 1:24), had to gain wisdom. He wasn't inherently born with it. He had to gain it the same way we do. This same principle applies to seeing in the Spirit. We have the ability to approach the Father the same way he did. Jesus said to Nathanael in John 1:50-51 (ESV), "'You will see greater things than these.' And he said to him, 'Truly, truly, I say to you, you will see heaven opened, and the angels of God ascending and descending on the Son of Man.'"

This promise is available to any and all who are in Christ. Any eyes that have been opened by the Father and have put their faith in Jesus now have this privilege! It's a promise from God. Acts 2:17 (TPT) says,

> *This is what I will do in the last days—I will pour out my Spirit on everybody and cause your sons and daughters to prophesy, and your young men will see visions, and your old men will experience dreams from God.*

He will pour his Spirit out on "everybody" - not just a select few. The result will be an awakening, and it keeps growing more and more to this day. A glorious ability to see visions in the Holy Spirit. To dream dreams that come from the heart of God.

He's not saying that young men will be the only ones to see visions and the old men will be the only ones to dream dreams. He's using a type of speech to give examples of what will happen. All of it is for "everyone!" Anyone who has received the Holy Spirit has the ability to gaze upon the Son of Man.

There are different types of visions and seeing in the Spirit. Occurrences ranging from Peter on the rooftop, Paul on the road to Damascus, Stephen while being stoned, John on the island of Patmos, and many others.

I used to think that real "Holy Spirit inspired visions" were ones like the examples I just mentioned. It had to be a crazy intense situation. I thought I had to see things in the

Spirit with my physical eyes (like Stephen) in order for it to count as a vision. I figured *real* visions from God were so powerful that I'd be left temporarily blind (like Paul). I would have to be wondering if I was in my body or out of my body when the vision occurred (like John).

While these types of visions are amazing, they are not the only way we have Holy Spirit inspired visions. It's not the only way to see Jesus and gaze upon heavenly realities. Nathanael is a perfect example of this.

THE WORD

Let's keep this simple. The Word tells us to fix our thoughts on things that are above (Colossians 3:2). His Word gives us a glimpse into God and what his Kingdom is like. John 1:14 (ESV) says, "And the Word became flesh and dwelt among us, and we have seen his glory, glory as of the only Son from the Father, full of grace and truth."

Notice that this verse says the Word became *flesh*. It doesn't say the Word became *text*! What I'm saying is that the Bible is intended to lead us to an encounter with the living Christ. It's not just basic instructions before leaving earth (B.I.B.L.E.). It is far more than a manual! It is alive and active! Hebrews 4:12 (ESV) says,

> *For the word of God is living and active, sharper than any two-edged sword, piercing to the division of soul and of spirit, of joints and of marrow, and discerning the thoughts and intentions of the heart.*

The Lord does not want us to use the Word as a rule book or something only to gain knowledge. The intent of the knowledge is to lead us to relationship with Jesus through the habitation of the Holy Spirit. Jesus said this to the Pharisees in John 6:63 (TPT), "The Holy Spirit is the one who gives life, that which is of the natural realm is of no help. The words I speak to you are Spirit and life. But there are still some of you who won't believe." And in John 5:39-40 (TPT) he says,

> *You are busy analyzing the Scriptures, frantically poring over them in hopes of gaining eternal life. Everything you read points to me, yet you still refuse to come to me so I can give you the life you're looking for - eternal life!*

His Word gives our minds a clear picture for us to see heavenly realities. Let's go through some examples of what this could look like.

If anger is something that has a grip on your life (this has been one of mine) and you have trouble with self-control, then begin to renew your mind with the Word. Get filled with specific words from God in Scripture and let your mind paint the truths in your thoughts. Gaze upon the truth.

For example, I would begin to think about how Jesus responded to people in frustrating situations. His death on the cross was one that easily could have angered him. I would close my eyes and visualize him hanging on the cross while his murderers hurled insults at him. I know in the Word how he responded to all of these people - in love. In my mind, I would play through all the different interactions he had with people on the cross and keep in my mind that he refrained from acting in rage during all of the events.

I take that example and I then receive it for myself. I see him treating me that way. I look at my own mistakes I've made out of anger and I begin to visualize his reaction to me. My old way of thinking was that he was frustrated with me. He furrowed his eyebrows and rolled his eyes at me. He'd let out a deep sigh as if I was such a bother and annoyance to him.

Shouldn't he feel that way? It was another one of the many same exact mistakes I had made time and time again. Couldn't I learn my lesson? How many times was I going to let the same mistake happen? I must have been wearing his patience thin.

No, this was not the truth at all. I was using my thoughts and imagination to receive lies regarding his feelings toward me. I began to get a picture of the real truth. How he really feels and responds to my failures is in his Word. Matthew 18:22 says that Jesus instructed his disciples to forgive a person seventy times seven times in one day. Certainly, Jesus wouldn't command us to do something that he wouldn't do himself.

I began to see him display radical patience and forgiveness toward me in my thoughts. The same reaction he had toward his murderers on the cross - he has for me. What's happening is I'm seeing God in correct alignment to who he is and how he operates. In the process of letting truth renew my mind, I'm simultaneously learning to do what he does, just like Jesus said would happen in John 5:19. I begin to do what I see the Father doing.

Let's look at fear. Perhaps you have a fear of sudden death coming upon you or a loved one. Some say we have no control over things like that, and it's all in God's hands. But is that really what his Word says? Psalm 91:9-10 (ESV) says, "Because you have made the Lord your dwelling place—the Most High, who is my refuge—no evil shall be allowed to befall you, no plague come near your tent."

Gaze upon this heavenly reality. See yourself coming before him. See him being the strength and trust of your life. Imagine yourself in years to come seeking him and his Kingdom first. If you feel you can't say he is the dwelling place and refuge of your life, then start to see it happening. You are making him your dwelling place and you are growing in it.

When difficult seasons come, see yourself running to him. When you make mistakes and lean on your own understanding, see him coming to rescue you from the trouble. David wrote in Psalm 27:4 (ESV), "One thing have I asked of the Lord, that will I seek after: that I may dwell in the house of the Lord all the days of my life, to gaze upon the beauty of the Lord and to inquire in his temple." Immediately following that verse, Psalm 27:5 (ESV) says, "For he will hide me in his shelter in the day of trouble; he will conceal me under the cover of his tent; he will lift me high upon a rock."

There is a correlation between dwelling with the Lord and gazing upon him. Then, there is a correlation between gazing upon the Lord and gaining confidence that we will be sheltered by him. Does the Bible promise no hardship or persecution will ever come our way? No, Jesus actually tells us we will experience these things. However, if we hide ourselves in him then he will be a fortress, shelter, and refuge in our days of trouble. And he promises even that calamity or tragedy will not come to our tent (our households and lives).

Using the Word to gaze upon the Lord helps us behold his true nature and we correct false projections of who he is in our minds. Lies get exposed and truths take their place. Does that mean everything changes for us immediately? Not necessarily - but don't be surprised if it does!

One thing to note regarding the importance of the Word is that using it helps us keep our minds in line with the truth. For instance, if we are gazing upon him and we see something like Jesus dying a second time, we have the Word to correct and instruct us. Hebrews 10:12 (NIV) tells us, "But when this priest had offered for all time one sacrifice for sins, he sat down at the right hand of God." Not only does the Word give us truth to gaze upon, it corrects any false ideas that may come from something other than the heart of God.

FAITH

Another requirement to seeing him in the Spirit is faith. Without faith it's impossible to please God. In fact, Romans 14:23 (TPT) says, "For anything we do that doesn't spring from faith is, by definition, sinful." Hebrews 11:6 (ESV) says, "And without faith it is impossible to please him, for whoever would draw near to God must believe that he exists and that he rewards those who seek him."

Wow. The importance of faith. God wants our entire lives to be lived from a place of faith. The context of Hebrews 11:6 is that God desires us to have a clear conscience in living for him. I'm not saying that if we don't take time to gaze upon Jesus then we are living in sin.

Nothing of this book is a "have to." There's no legal requirement for those who are in Christ. We don't have to do anything, but we *get to* do everything that's the desire and will of God. We don't have to gaze upon him but we are crowned with the privilege to do so as sons and daughters.

By saying faith is a requirement, I'm highlighting that if we doubt in our hearts that we can see heavenly realities, then we will be in a constant struggle. Our times of seeking him will be filled with questions and confusion of if what is happening is real. Questioning our experiences isn't necessarily wrong, because authenticity is a good thing to desire. However, we have to be careful because at times a desire to be authentic can actually be a mask covering up

When we gaze upon the Lord
we behold his true nature
and we correct false projections
of who he is in our minds.

what's really going on inside: doubt and unbelief.

Let's look at this from a practical example. I used to work at a desk. From my desk I could see outside. I remember one time looking out the window, and across the highway there was a home improvement store. I was looking at the store and the different architecture of it. I was admiring the type of materials they used to make the building because it was unique to its competitors. And if I'm being honest I was a bit bored and was wasting time at work. I mean, I was staring at a building. How bored do you have to be to do that?

The store has outer walls made of concrete with vertical lines. The concrete on the walls is rough, not smooth at all. The roof is a forest green color and the building itself is large, rectangular in shape. I'd say it's around 500 feet wide and 300 feet deep; around the same size of a Walmart or Costco.

From what I just described, you have a general understanding of the store. If you and I were to compare the different images in our minds, they'd be different in some ways but the same in others. If I asked you if you believed it was a real place, you'd say yes because you have no reason to believe that I'm lying to you.

This is the same process we can have when we are gazing upon the Lord. We read his Word to get an accurate picture of truth, and in faith we believe what's happening is real. We are only seeing in part, but just because we only see a glimpse doesn't mean that it's not real.

Let's take the same example but apply it to seeing into heavenly places. Let's read through some verses that describe what he is like and how he interacts with us. Revelation 4:2-3 (ESV) says,

At once I was in the Spirit, and behold, a throne stood in

heaven, with one seated on the throne. And he who sat there had the appearance of jasper and carnelian, and around the throne was a rainbow that had the appearance of an emerald.

Pause here and see this place in your mind. Know that it's real and what you are seeing isn't just your imagination. It's not just fantasy or a projection you are seeing in your thoughts. Since you are seated with Christ in heavenly places, through faith you are currently there.

His eyes are like a flame of fire, and on his head are many diadems, and he has a name written that no one knows but himself. He is clothed in a robe dipped in blood, and the name by which he is called is The Word of God. (Revelation 19:12-13, ESV)

Pause and use these verses to gaze upon him. Don't move on until you believe in faith that what you are seeing is reality.

Zechariah 2:8 (NKJV) says, "for he who touches you touches the apple of his eye." See him reaching his hand out to touch you. His fingers make contact with you, confirming that he is calling you the apple of his eye. You are the one he finds great delight in. Rest here and meditate before going to the next verse.

Zephaniah 3:17 (ESV) says, "The Lord your God is in your midst, a mighty one who will save; he will rejoice over you with gladness; he will quiet you by his love; he will exult over you with loud singing." Gaze at the gladness on his face as he rejoices over you. Fears and anxieties are silenced by his love. A mighty roar of singing comes forth from his mouth. From inside the depths of his heart comes a song.

Rest and hear the song he has for you.

These are just a few examples of how we gaze upon Jesus. We've partnered the Word with our faith and had an encounter with him. I encourage you to make this a regular routine. This will take your friendship with him to new levels and you will be transformed by the renewing of your mind. This is key to creating a vibrant and consistent secret place with God in your life. Gazing upon Jesus keeps us wanting more. It helps make time with God a natural habit.

SOUND DOCTRINE

As we use the Word of God and our faith to meet with the Lord, there's a need for sound doctrine - especially when it comes to Old Testament passages. There are many verses in the Old Testament that express God's method of handling the sin of his people. It's imperative that we learn and gain wisdom on what verses of the Old Testament apply to us now and what verses don't, now that we are living in the New Covenant.

For example, several times we read about God executing judgment on his people and punishing them in the Old Testament. However, through Jesus' work on the cross we know that he took the punishment for us. Any visualization that we see of God condemning us for our actions is incorrect because the Word of God tells us how he deals with us under the New Covenant. This is where gaining wisdom and insight come into play.

Gazing upon Jesus keeps us wanting more. It helps make time with God a natural habit.

REFLECTION

Use the space provided below and on the next page to reflect on what the Lord showed you during the exercises on pages 82 - 84.

REFLECTION

(continued space to reflect, express,
and digest what the Lord is showing you)

CHAPTER 6

LIVING INSIDE OUT

Beholding Jesus has powerful implications to igniting our secret place time with God but it doesn't stop there. Seeing Jesus has a direct impact on how we live our lives before men too. It is an engine that fuels evangelism in our lives.

Genesis tells us that God walked with Adam and Eve in the Garden of Eden. Ever since The Fall, he has been working to bring that reality back to existence. Let's look at what the Lord has done to restore our relationship with him throughout the past 6,000 years.

Man became separated from God and God then worked to create a physical dwelling place where he could meet with Man again. After that, God became a man and dwelt among us. Then, he made a way to dwell inside Man through the Holy Spirit.

It's amazing that you and I have been strategically placed in his perfectly orchestrated and unfolding plan. Every step of his salvation and reconciliation plan has gotten us closer and closer to him.

Over the years, I've become more enthralled at the glorious riches I have because of the Holy Spirit dwelling inside me. Jesus told the disciples it would be better for them when he left and ascended into heaven because then the Holy Spirit would come (John 16:7).

How could this be?

What could be better than living with the physical and tangible presence of God? Perhaps Jesus was just trying to make them feel better in a difficult moment. No way! Jesus never told a lie, and if he said it would be better, well, then it has to be better. Not just as good - he said better! A problem is that most Christians and even Christian leaders have a very limited perspective on what it means to be indwelt by the Holy Spirit.

I'm so thankful to live in this time God has us in. I used to say things like, "I wish I was born when Jesus walked the earth. Then, I could have walked with him and seen him!" I don't say that anymore. It's not that it is a bad thing to say, but it minimizes the reality of God living in us. It makes little of the depth of friendship and intimacy we can have with God through the Holy Spirit.

We get to dwell with God 24/7 through the Holy Spirit. We don't face a lot of the challenges the disciples faced. No physical limitations. No schedule conflicts. No geographical obstructions. Complete, perfect, harmonious fellowship with Jesus, anytime and anywhere. It truly is better! But the pleasures of knowing Christ through communion with the Holy Spirit don't stop with us. Beholding Jesus in the secret place has a direct impact on the knowledge of the glory of the Lord spreading through the earth.

ANOTHER LOOK AT THE RIVER OF LIFE

In chapter three, we looked at the river of life. Let's elaborate more on that topic. To refresh your memory, we learned how the river of life flows from the throne of God, through the city of God, and then to the spirit of Man. One of the verses we looked at was John 7:38 (ESV) which says, "Whoever believes in me, as the Scripture has said, 'Out of his heart will flow rivers of living water.'"

We learned that the river begins to flow out of our spirits, into our souls, and then out of our bodies. The same question I posed in chapter three I ask now: is that where the river of life stops? Does the river of life stop flowing after it bubbles up to our bodies? Let's look at Habakkuk 2:14 (NIV) for that answer. It says, "For the earth will be filled with the knowledge of the glory of the Lord as the waters cover the sea."

I used to think that this prophetic declaration was just a nice visual representation of the knowledge of the glory of the Lord. I've learned that there is more to it than that. There's a connection between these two verses mentioned.

God's plan has always been to dwell with Man and we are now the dwelling places of God. And as the dwelling places of God, he has chosen us to be the outflow of the river of life that will cover the earth. He will truly come again on the clouds. There is coming a time when everyone will see him in his fullness and all will have the knowledge that Christ is Lord. There's no doubt about that.

However, in the season we are in now, the knowledge of the glory of the Lord is flooding the earth like the waters cover the sea. And we are the streams by which he is accomplishing this. When we behold Jesus and gaze upon him, his river of life flows freely through us and is unleashed into the world. Our lives begin to shine the light of God for the whole world to see. His river flows out and covers the earth like the waters cover the sea.

THE OVERFLOWING LIGHT

At the end of chapter four, we looked at Jesus' teaching called "The Eye is the Lamp of the Body." We learned that the eye he is referencing is actually the "inner eye" of our understanding and thoughts. We discussed that seeing (desiring) the world fills us with darkness and seeing God fills us with light. We also know that light's natural ability is to illuminate. But there's more to this lesson. Jesus says in Luke 8:16-18 (TPT),

> *No one lights a lamp and then hides it, covering it over or putting it where its light won't be seen. No, the lamp is placed on a lamp stand so others are able to benefit from its brightness. Because this revelation lamp now shines within you, nothing will be hidden from you—it will all be revealed. Every secret of the kingdom will be unveiled and out in the open, made known by the revelation-light.*
>
> *So pay careful attention to your hearts as you hear my teaching, for to those who have open hearts, even more revelation will be given to them until it overflows. And for those who do not listen with open hearts, what little light they imagine to have will be taken away.*

We know that our eyes are the lamp of the body and we first get filled with light by beholding and gazing upon Jesus. It happens by seeing him and believing the truth of who he is. But it doesn't stop there. Jesus wants to pour the light of who he is from his dwelling place (our spirits), into our souls (our mind, will, and emotions), and then let it spill into our Outer Courts. Our physical bodies are the Outer Courts of his dwelling place and they are also the place where God outputs his light into the world. It's our actions that bring forth the light of God into the world.

WE ARE PRIESTS OF GOD'S TEMPLE

We know that in the Old Testament, the Levites were the priests who would perform the different duties of the temple. During the time of sacrifice, a priest would begin at the Outer Court.

He would sacrifice the offering, then move toward the Holy Place. After performing different requirements there, he would enter into the Holy of Holies. Looking at this process in its simplest form, we see that the priests would start from the outside and work their way in. Now, under the New Covenant, that process has in a way been reversed. Let's look at a few different points to support that claim.

1. Jesus performed the final earthly sacrifice for us.

His Word says that he entered into the temple of God as the sacrifice himself. After giving his life, he entered all the way into the Holy of Holies before Father God. There he sat down as our high priest. When he sat down as high priest it meant there would no longer be a need for sacrifices as described in Old Covenant law. His blood is eternal and there can be no sacrifice greater than him.

Therefore, there is no need to make sacrifices before

God as a means to atone for sin and be made right with him. In other words, there is no reason to believe that we are ever apart from God. And since we are never apart from him, there's no "outside to inside" process anymore. Yes, we can draw near him as James 4:8 says, but we have to consider also that we are always with him. He has promised to never leave or forsake us. James 4:8 is telling us to seek and pursue him above all other things.

If something takes his place on the throne of our hearts, then there is a time to enter in through confession and repentance. But the default way in which we live is from the Holy of Holies. The only continual and ongoing sacrifice left to make is the one of thankfulness and praise.

2. We are spirit beings first and everything flows from there.

We know that we are now the temple of God and he dwells inside our spirits. Our spirits are the core of us. We are eternal beings and while our bodies are a significant part, everything begins at the spirit level.

In the Old Testament temple, the priests started from the outside and worked their way in. In the New Testament, we start from the inside and work our way out. Intimacy with God can now be as instantaneous as we believe it to be. It's something that we naturally walk in 24/7, regardless of what we feel and how good of a person we are. We are seated with Christ in heavenly places. There's no need to work something up. No need to wait for a feeling.

We live from the place of sonship and it's from that place of sonship that the Spirit and glory of God flows to our mind, will, and emotions. And from there, it flows through our actions. Trying to live "good enough" to be right with God has so many things wrong with it. Christ already lived the perfect life for us.

Now, the priestly duties have been reversed. Good works flow from a place of sonship. It flows from gazing upon Jesus - a place of constant friendship and fellowship. It's not something we have to work up or earn. We simply recognize that we are one with him and we walk with him. In the process, he works with us and matures us.

We may start small, but he patiently guides us in this lifestyle of communion and gazing upon him. We may find it difficult to walk in the Spirit like this because of things like shame, trying to be good enough, guilt, sin, etc. However, all of these are things that Jesus has unlimited mercy toward. He knows us and our weaknesses. We just have to keep our eyes on him.

3. The veil has been torn.

At Jesus' death, the earth shook and inside the temple the veil that separated the Holy Place and the Holy of Holies ripped in two. It's no longer just ordained priests who enter into the Holy of Holies, but anyone can through Jesus.

I'd like to submit that it's not the only benefit we received. The torn veil also signifies the free flowing river of life that naturally flows out of the bellies of believers into the Outer Courts of the world. The torn veil signifies free access into the presence of God as well as free distribution of the presence of God into the world. Healing, signs and wonders, miracles, reconciliation, and more are all readily available to anyone who believes.

WE ARE WITNESSES

Let's keep diving further into this reality that we are the

temples of God and have access to meet with him anytime, anywhere. We have the glorious privilege to gaze upon him and to behold the beauty of the Lord in his temple at all times.

If we are living in the natural flow of walking in the Spirit, then his light is flooding our souls and bodies. And if he is flooding out of us, then witnessing will be automatic. It will become an unforced lifestyle.

Witnessing should be a natural overflow from seeing the transfigured Jesus. It should be so easy for us that if Jesus didn't want us to tell others about him, then he'd have to ask us not to. There are stories of Jesus having to specifically tell people not to go and tell others of what he did in their lives.

- In Matthew 17, Jesus tells Peter, James, and John not to tell anyone what happened on the Mount of Transfiguration until the proper timing.

- In Mark 1 and Luke 5, Jesus tells a man he heals of leprosy not to tell anyone that it was Jesus who healed him.

- In Mark 5, Jesus resurrects a little girl and tells her parents not to tell anyone of the event.

The point is that Jesus knew their natural response from the miracles that he did would be to tell others about it. Whatever the reason behind Jesus telling them to not tell others we can leave for others to discuss. But there's one point that everyone can agree on. When we get around Jesus and witness who he is and what he does, the natural response will be to go and tell others about it!

A big reason why evangelism is so hard at times is because we are doing it from a sense of obligation. We feel that since Jesus commissioned us to do it then we have to do it. There's also a fear in us that if we don't witness and evangelize, it's because we're ashamed of him. Neither of those ideas are motivated by love.

I know because I've been there.

I used to make myself evangelize and in doing so I force-fed people the gospel. I just assumed the awkwardness was a part of the process. I would get charged up as a "good Christian soldier" and strike up awkward conversations with friends and coworkers. I wouldn't say that's the wrong way to do it, but it's certainly not the best way to do it.

My problem was that I wasn't sharing with them from an overflow of what I had witnessed of him in my own personal life. I would share testimonies of what he'd done in my life in the past, but it was as if I was just reciting a story. There was something lacking, and I believe it was in those times that I was missing nearness to him.

I wasn't witnessing from a place of constant communion with Jesus. It was just about telling people of past events. It was missing the simple, genuine, natural response of having beheld him. God wants us to behold him in all his beauty, and then from that experience, go and share the good news.

He wants us to tell others with a heart of gratitude, thanks, and faith. When this happens, the past stories we tell become infused with the glory and fragrance of Christ. It doesn't mean everyone will receive our message, but it definitely helps put them in a better position to do so.

In its simplest form, a witness is someone who tells others what he or she saw. In the court of law, when witnesses share a life-changing event they saw, you can see it on their faces. When they revisit that moment, something happens to their countenance. When they share their story, you can see it on their face. It's like they're reliving the moment all over again. They're not just reciting the event that took place.

That's the essence of what I'm talking about. How can we tell others about Jesus Christ from a place of having *been there*? We want to share about him to others as if we have just beheld him in his glory. It's not wrong to share our testimonies as a past event, but God wants us to be so presently full of him that when we share, it's as natural as it was for the woman at the well (John 4:1-42).

I believe that's what many Christians are missing when it comes to evangelism. It's not that they need to force an emotional expression, but when beholding Jesus happens there's going to be an eyes-wide-open, heart-transforming type of experience. And it's primarily those consistent, love-tsunami type encounters that our witnessing should be motivated by.

If there is little to no personal witnessing of Jesus happening in our lives, how can we expect witnessing to others about Jesus to go over well? Acts 1:8 (TPT) says,

> *But I promise you this—the Holy Spirit will come upon you and you will be filled with power. And you will be my messengers (witnesses) to Jerusalem, throughout Judea, the distant provinces — even to the remotest places on earth!*

Acts 2:4 (TPT) says, "They were all filled and equipped with the Holy Spirit…" The book of Acts tells us there is a strong correlation between being filled with the Holy Spirit and then going out as witnesses of the good news. When we put our faith in Jesus, the Holy Spirit comes to reside within us.

In that sense, all believers are filled with the Holy Spirit. However, witnessing isn't something that automatically happens once we're saved. When it happens, most of us naturally want to tell others. But many of us know that unless we are continually tapping into the flow of the Holy Spirit, telling others about Jesus gets difficult and burdensome over time.

Living from a lifestyle of nearness with Jesus helps us to continue to access the rivers of life that are within us; and in turn, the river of life flows naturally out of us. It flows out in the way we talk and in the way we conduct ourselves. When his river is flowing from our spirits to our souls and then our bodies, there's an amazing process happening. It's the natural process of evangelism.

If there is little to no personal witnessing of Jesus happening in our lives, how can we expect witnessing to others about Jesus to go over well?

REFLECTION

Spend some time reflecting on these questions. Use the space provided to journal and write down what the Holy Spirit is speaking to you.

1. What are some struggles you have had with evangelism?

2. Have you had any experiences with God like the ones in the Bible where the people were so touched by God they couldn't resist telling others? If so, reflect, remember, and write about it.

3. My hope is that our prayer time would be filled with the pleasures of knowing Christ and that witnessing would be a natural response to what we see. Take some time to gaze upon Jesus and Kingdom realities. What do you see and experience?

REFLECTION

Use the space provided below to write any personal revelations you've received. Write down words, phrases, or desires that are stirred within you. You can draw pictures that you may have seen in your mind while reading this chapter. This is a blank canvas to express your heart.

CHAPTER 7

BREAKING FREE

I have experienced many ups and downs in my relationship with Jesus. I know what it's like to have consistent time with the Lord, and I know what it's like to put it low on my priority list. I know what it's like to "pray without ceasing," and I know what it's like to go long periods of time without even acknowledging him.

I know what it's like to follow through with my Bible reading plan and what it's like to totally fail at it. I know what it is to have plenty of head knowledge about God but to totally miss letting him transform my heart.

The hills and valleys of following Jesus have helped me gain a much better understanding of the height, depth, length, and width of his love. I, like all of us, have plenty more to learn, but I would like to share some things that helped me in my personal walk with Jesus. Specifically, I'd like to éxpose some of the obstacles of legalism and lies that can come against us in regards to having personal time with the Lord.

TIME WITH GOD

Time with God is a common term I've used in this book and it's a term used in many Christian circles. It's a simple, easy to understand way of describing what we desire at the core of us. We're after communion and deep fellowship with God. Jesus modeled it for us, and in order for us to seek him this way, there's going to be some amount of time required. It's completely logical for us to call *time with God* exactly what it is: *time with God*.

However, the problem with that phrase is that we can very quickly turn *time with God* into a checklist activity. It's common in Western culture to set goals as a way to create progress in our lives. We make very detailed schedules of our day to get every minute out of it that we possibly can. In terms of efficiency, it's a great thing. However, in terms of relationship, it's a different story.

We have to be careful to not turn connecting deeply with Jesus into a task or chore.

How would my wife or children feel if every time I was with them I looked at my watch to determine how much time I was obligated to spend with them? We have schedules, appointments, meetings, and commitments that we need to honor. It's not wrong to take care of these things and be mindful of them in our relationships. However, reducing our personal relationship with the magnificent, holy, perfect God to another item on our to do list just doesn't seem right.

I used to put *time with God* on my to do list and it was a good thing... for a season. It was during a time that proximity to him wasn't a priority. I needed discipline to help me make nearness to him more important in my life. The problem that arises with putting God on our to do list is the motivation behind it.

In my life, I remember going through countless attempts of spending time with God as a task to accomplish, not as an opportunity to delight in a friend. At some point I'd fail and feel like I'd disappointed God. Getting out of this trap of legalism was one of the most difficult things I've faced in walking with Jesus.

Let's expose the false requirement that we have to have *time with God*. Nowhere in the Bible does it tell us that we have to do it. Nowhere does it tell us how much time in a day we should spend with him. In fact, it doesn't even say that we're required to do it daily. I know that some may say that's borderline heresy. To say that seeking God personally isn't required of us has to be evil, right?

Some say that since the Israelites were instructed to get manna daily, then we should eat the manna that came from heaven (seek Jesus personally) daily. Others say that since Jesus told us to remember him as often as we eat (Luke 22:19 in the upper room), then we should have one-on-one communion with him three times a day.

The essence of these examples is that he is the bread of life and in order for us to truly live, we need to partake in a relationship with him. In order for our inner beings to truly live, a relationship with him is vitally important. It's as important as our bodies needing food to survive. Just like our bodies need food to live, so our inner being (soul and spirit) needs him to live. These passages aren't giving us rules and methods to follow; they are simply expressing the great need that we have to commune with Jesus.

While all these rules, methods, and requirements sound helpful and may certainly be a great way to set us up for personal encounters with Jesus, there's a snare and trap waiting if we aren't careful. The problem is that God never explicitly tells us how frequently we should be spending time alone with him. In fact, he never tells us that we have to spend time with him at all... ever. It may sound blasphemous but that's the Biblical reality.

Some of us don't like that idea because of fear that we'd abuse the freedom and live our lives short of his calling. The thought implies that we'd choose the things of this world over nearness with him. It views the power of grace, mercy, and the love of God as very weak in comparison to the power of sin. So we create rules for ourselves. We likely create them out of good intention, but then when we fail to meet them, we experience guilt, shame, and condemnation. The Pharisees were known to create their own rules too. In Matthew 15:9 (ESV), Jesus says, "...in vain do they worship me, teaching as doctrines the commandments of men."

Jesus is saying that these people created their own rules but treated them as if they were rules from God. These Pharisees were very different in their heart motives than most of us, but a principle we see from this is that they were creating their own rules. And we do this to ourselves a lot without even knowing it.

It's likely that many of these man-made teachings were created for the benefit of the people - ideas to help people walk in a way that was pleasing to the Lord. But the problem is there are strings attached to them. If we tell ourselves that we need to spend an hour each day with God and then fail to meet that standard, usually a slow, steady stream of guilt and disappointment sets in.

God doesn't require us to have time with him, but it's the best thing we can do for ourselves.

We tell ourselves things like, "I'll make up for it tomorrow" or "I'll do it later today." Inevitably, we at some point fail at achieving those goals and begin compounding the guilt and disappointment. In this process, we project these condemning thoughts onto God. Subconsciously (or even consciously) we believe that God is disappointed in us. We believe God has distanced himself from us. He's given us a cold shoulder and turned his eyes upon someone else who can better serve him.

The rules that were intended to bring us good actually ended up being the thing that brought strife. Strife that didn't come from God. These rules, when failed to be met, create disappointment that we put on ourselves that God never put on us. God doesn't put rules and time frames on our personal time with him because it's a relationship!

What would a friendship be if it revolved around only certain slots of time in our day? We can be walking with the Lord, letting him be a part of everything we do. That means during our work commutes, breakfast, lunch, dinner, our face-to-face time with him, and everywhere in between. He's not keeping track of how much or how little time we spend with him!

Time isn't the point of nearness - nearness is the point!

He's not putting guilt and condemnation on us when we don't make pursuing him a priority.

Don't get me wrong - if seeking him is not a priority, then there will be little to no fruit to come from our lives. I'm certainly *not* saying that seeking him isn't important. It's the most important thing we can do. Personal, one-on-one relationship with Jesus is the very thing that centers us. It should be the driving force and fuel for every believer's life. But even as important as it is, God will never make relationship with him a forced obligation motivated by performance, grit, and our own strength.

*The thing he wants to motivate us in pursuing him is **him**!*

Not our hard work and determination. Lovers don't have to force themselves to love each other. And that's what God wants between us. God didn't force himself to become a man, experience our struggles, and die for us! He was motivated by love. The truth of the matter is, if we stay focused on him and his nature, then there will be no need to put him on our to do list. He wants us to be so captivated and enamored with him that we can't *not* think about him.

Imagine someone who for a time is apart from her lover. She can't stop thinking about him and the overwhelming love inevitably motivates her to make a move to draw near him. She's going to find a way to "get away" from everything and see him. The bliss and ecstasy found in the relationship is too much to resist! It's too much to ignore and get out of her mind.

That's what God wants with us. It's when we start adding all the rules to the relationship that the relationship itself becomes lifeless and the Lord becomes distant to us. It's just like the laws of Moses. The Bible tells us that the law has no power to give life. It only has power to give death. It's not that the rules are bad, but they have no ability to bring us to life. They can only point to our great need of having a relationship with the Lord Jesus Christ so that we can become alive through knowing him.

The next time you start to feel bad about not spending time with the Lord, DON'T! It's a legalistic trap that will not spur you on to love him more. It will only create a performance-based relationship that depends on works, not the grace of God.

Throw out the timer entirely. Five minutes or five hours - that's not the point. The point is to enjoy him! To take great delight in the lover of your soul. The guilt, condemnation, and disappointment will not strengthen your relationship with God. And remember - he doesn't have those negative thoughts toward you! There is no condemnation for those who are in Christ Jesus. He's not shaming you, so don't bully yourself. We aren't doing God any favors by doing so. And that leads me to the next lie to be exposed.

SELF-BULLYING

Bullying is a common topic discussed these days, but the idea of self-bullying isn't talked about nearly as much. Self-bullying is far more common than bullying and it's something we don't even realize we do. It stems from toxic thoughts that we've had for so long and often that they happen without us even realizing it. Self-bullying drives many people to depression and anxiety. It causes social fears and pushes us to isolation.

It's also very common because it's not discouraged like person-to-person bullying is. Fortunately, there has been a rise of defenders to people who are being bullied. However, defending someone who is bullying him or herself is more difficult to do. How do you defend someone who is at war with themself? It's certainly possible but as Christians we aren't trained in how to do that very well.

A big challenge with self-bullying is that most of the toxic thoughts come from a distortion of the truth. It's called deception and it's the enemy's primary way of fooling us. If he can get us to believe a straight-up lie, he'll certainly deliver one to us. However, his most common way to deceive us is through half-truths. Half-truths are lies that have a form of truth. The enemy does this by twisting the Word of God.

The serpent told Adam and Eve a half-truth by twisting something God said in the garden and he deceived them. He tried to fool Jesus in the wilderness by using the Word of God, but he failed. The enemy knows that if we realize he is the one telling us the lie, then we won't believe it. However, if he can get us to believe God is the one saying it, then he knows we'll believe it.

How about you? Have you been tricked by the enemy through Scripture? Years after committing myself to the Lord, I remember reading through 1 John and being scared out of my mind that I wasn't saved. 1 John 3:6 (ESV) says, "No one who abides in him keeps on sinning; no one who keeps on sinning has either seen him or known him."

My problem was that I had loads of sin I was still dealing with in my life after being saved for several years. Since I had been a Christian for so long, maybe that meant I was never truly a Christian. If I was a real Christian, the sin should have stopped, right? Isn't that what 1 John 3:6 says?

Maybe I was destined to be raised up to be an object of God's wrath like Pharaoh (Romans 9:22). These are the types of Biblically-based questions that would haunt me. It wasn't until I began to have a deeper understanding of 1 John 3:6 that my eyes were illuminated by the truth and purpose of that verse.

This verse isn't saying that if we struggle with sin, then we're not going to heaven. He's showing us that the way to stop sinning is to abide in him. He's saying it's impossible to keep sinning if you have seen him and known him. Therefore, if we are sinning then we should draw near to him because that's how it will inevitably stop. It's an invitation to draw near to God - to see and encounter him.

If we're still struggling with sin, then we should

evaluate our *relationship with him*, not our *salvation in him*. He's not drawing a line in the sand. He's not saying, "Either clean up your act or I'll cast you into darkness." His Word says that it's his will and desire that none perish. Hebrews 4:15-16 (ESV) says,

> *For we do not have a high priest who is unable to sympathize with our weaknesses, but one who in every respect has been tempted as we are, yet without sin. Let us then with confidence draw near to the throne of grace, that we may receive mercy and find grace to help in time of need.*

This is just one of the many examples from my own life that shows how self-bullying, as it relates to our faith in Christ, can happen. It tries to hide itself in the Word of God because if it can, it then becomes very hard to uproot from our belief system. The enemy knows how powerful the Word is. If he can distort it enough and twist the truth into a lie, then he can deceive believers and they won't even realize it because they think it's the true Word of God.

It's imperative for us to have a deep revelation of the grace, mercy, and love of God. Revelation that can only come through seeing and knowing him. That way when the enemy tries to fool us, we have loads and loads of personal encounters with the Person of truth. The truth defends against the lies that come against us in our minds.

When our minds have been feasting on the pure truth of God's nature toward us, it makes it that much easier to know how he feels toward us when the lies come. He expresses love and sympathy, like Hebrews 4:15-16 explains. Then, the truth of how he feels toward us floods into the thoughts we have toward ourselves and the self-bullying begins to cease.

It's possible, too, that self-bullying can be the

motivating factor behind someone bullying someone else. Negative thoughts, words, and beliefs flow through our minds and we become burdened by them. Someone struggling with these inner thoughts can begin projecting these same hurtful words and thoughts onto others. A bully has a poor self-image and in order to cope with the inner torment, the bully tears down others. As the saying goes, hurt people hurt people.

That poor self-image with all the critical thoughts and self-destructive phrases spoken over oneself usually started from lies coming from another person. And the person who said the hurtful words probably said them because of the same inner pain that the person they just bullied now feels. It's a poison and cancer meant to destroy the true image God has created us to have through the reconciling work of Jesus Christ.

THE PERFECT ENVIRONMENT

I've looked back on my life and noticed something that I realized needed some changing. And that is that most of my times with God happened during a controlled environment around me. Many of our church services are filled with amazing lights, productions, music, etc. As a person who, as you've probably figured out by now, abhors legalism and man-made rules because of how they "distract from pure and simple devotion to Christ" (2 Corinthians 11:3), I will be quick to say these things *are not* bad.

People who say these things distract from Jesus are experiencing their own inner obstacles and barriers they need to overcome. However, I do think these things can condition our souls into believing that in order for us to have deep fellowship with God we need to have an influenced environment around us.

And that's just simply not true.

Did Jesus have an amazing light display to help him "see what the Father was doing" whenever he would withdraw from the crowds to be with his dad? No, of course not. Lights weren't invented yet and even if they were... c'mon, just no.

When Peter, James, and John ascended the Mount of Transfiguration with Jesus, was the Hillsong worship team hanging out on the side to provide the perfect song to help them see the transfigured Jesus shining in all his radiant light? The answer is no.

I'll reiterate that I have no problem with these outer influences. They are in many ways Biblical and can be beautiful displays of worship to him. But if we find ourselves requiring them in order to have intimate nearness with the Lord, then we're improperly relying on them. In turn, it will result in countless missed divine moments of beholding God in our lives. As we learn to seek him in spirit and truth and not soul and truth, this becomes much easier and much more natural for us.

The truth that I most commonly use to approach him in spirit is that he likes me. The fact that he takes *great* delight in me. Literally, several times throughout my day I just stop and reflect on how much he enjoys me. I see him taking delight in me and I respond by seeing myself take delight in him. I might see him approach me with a smile on his face. He moves his hands behind my head and gently presses his forehead against mine. He gazes into me with his loving eyes of fire.

It's just simple relationship interaction that helps me keep my mind on him and the truth of who he is in our friendship. That's usually the way I first engage with him in personal prayer and worship. Is there worship music playing or the perfect light setup? Sometimes. Those things are nice but not necessary.

So don't feel like these things are bad or that you are not a mature Christian if you like having a setup environment to come before him. Definitely keep doing it! Just start the process of enjoying him outside of those times too.

OBEDIENCE

Alright, I'm going to say something that's probably going to stretch you and that is this...

Obedience is not a prerequisite to communion.

Now, before anyone goes and makes a website or blog to call me a heretic, just give me a second to defend that statement. I, by no means, take obedience to the Lord Jesus Christ lightly. I remember the times of my life that I lived in blatant and intentional disobedience to him.

I remember in prayer once telling him, "Lord, if you tell me to do what I don't want, I'm not listening and won't obey." Those are some of the most evil words I've ever let run through my mind. I still even struggle at times with the regret of grieving the Holy Spirit. I wish I could go back and redo those seasons of my life, but Philippians 3:13 (TPT) is continually renewing my mind. That verse says, "I don't depend on my own strength to accomplish this; however I do have one compelling focus: I forget all of the past as I fasten my heart to the future instead."

I don't take obedience to the King of kings lightly. He is worthy of everything. Everything that we are and that we have. When we live in disobedience our lives go haywire.

There's just no way around it. He is God and it's in the DNA of all creation to obey him. Every knee will bow and every tongue will confess that HE is Lord. It's no wonder that, when we live in disobedience, we often feel like we aren't worthy to come before him.

However, coming before him is the only way for us to correctly align our lives into obedience. Just before and during Christ's crucifixion, all of the disciples sinned against him. Judas betrayed him, Peter denied him, and the rest of them deserted him. They all sought to save their own lives and sinned against Jesus.

But who were the ones who continued to work out their salvation? The ones who remained. Yes, they ran initially but when the Lord approached them after the resurrection, they stayed. In fact, when Peter realized it was Jesus on the shore speaking to them, he jumped out of the boat to swim to him because he knew he could get to him faster than the boat!

It's vital that even when we are living at the worst of our worst, we remain in him. We must continue to seek and pursue him. No matter how hypocritical we feel. No matter how dishonest it may seem. No matter how terrible our decision was. It's in his presence that we find the grace and strength to get delivered from our disobedient nature. Running and hiding from communion is the last thing we should do.

Bob Sorge says it well regarding holiness. He talks about the idea that holiness for God is inherent, but for Man it is derived. Therefore, holiness is a proximity issue for us.

We cannot become holy and free from sin apart from the presence of God. *The absence of sin cannot create the presence of Jesus, but the consistent presence of Jesus will create the absence of sin.*

The blood of Jesus is strong enough to bring us before

Abba, Father even in the middle of our weakest times. This doesn't give us a license to sin, but it gives us permission to get to the only place that we can get free from it! Nearness to him delivers us from a situation that has us postured in disobedience.

As we come before him, the holy blaze of fire that he is burns up everything that is not of him. He will comfort us with his love and our eyes will begin to see that he is a far better reward than whatever else is tempting us. As we gaze upon him and take great delight in him, all of a sudden that sin struggle becomes much less of a struggle.

Most of the time, we try to overcome sin through our own effort and strength. That's extremely hard to do. Really, even if we do overcome sin through our own ability, it usually creates some degree of self-righteousness anyway. And God calls our own righteousness as clean as used tampons (Isaiah 64:6)!

Another term for this pitfall is "spiritual time-out." For many of us, as children, when we disobeyed we were put into time-out. Now, I've done time-outs with all four of my children and they can be necessary at times. But really we don't see anything like this in the Bible, certainly not on this side of the New Covenant.

I cannot stress this point enough. If you have sinned or are living in sin, keep coming to him in spirit and truth. He sympathizes with you in your weakness and wants to provide a way out of it for you.

IMAGINATION

There's a myth and lie that people say too often and that is this: "I don't have a good imagination." All of us have great, God-given imaginations that the Lord wants to do amazing things with. When we say and believe that we don't have good imaginations, we are already setting ourselves up to have very few visions from the Lord.

You have a great, God-given imagination. He wants to paint heavenly, truth-filled realities onto the canvas of your mind. Get filled with the Word of God, believe in faith, and let his heavenly realities become infused in your thought life.

REFLECTION

Spend some time reflecting on these questions. Use the space provided to journal and write down what the Holy Spirit is speaking to you.

1. What are some of the lies and legalistic traps you have been snared into believing?

2. Are there any other lies or legalistic traps not mentioned in this chapter that you see in your life? If so, write them down and speak/listen to the Lord regarding them.

3. Is there an area of your life that you are living in disobedience to the Lord? If so, spend some time in his presence and let him tenderly love and speak to you. Write or draw what's happening.

REFLECTION

Use the space provided below to write any personal revelations you've received. Write down words, phrases, or desires that are stirred within you. You can draw pictures that you may have seen in your mind while reading this chapter. This is a blank canvas to express your heart.

CHAPTER 8

FINAL ENCOURAGEMENT

My hope is that the Word of God and the experiences the Lord has led me through have encouraged you to seek him in a way you never have before. Some of the things mentioned in this book may challenge and stretch your thinking. If that is the case, then I'd like to respond with this: *good*.

Whenever we are growing it's very normal to go through growing pains. It feels uncomfortable. We have lots of questions like, "Is there something wrong with me?" and "Is this supposed to be happening?" All of those questions are normal and a part of the process. I must encourage you to not be afraid of the things of the Spirit. You may have heard stories of people moving in the Holy Spirit in ways that seemed weird. There are a few things to remember in the process of following the Holy Spirit.

THE ONLY PERSON'S WORSHIP WE SHOULD BE JUDGING IS OUR OWN

When someone begins to experience the process of beholding God and gazing upon the Son of Man, it will very likely result in some form of outward expression of worship. As I mentioned in this book, the Bible says that the river of life flows out of us. This means there will be all sorts of beautiful expressions of worship ranging from extension of hands, dancing, shouting, kneeling, singing, etc. as a response to seeing Jesus in our hearts.

But it's not limited to the creative genre of worship. We can also worship him by helping someone move, giving a ride to a friend who needs help, giving someone money, etc. There's a very wide range of outward expressions of worship, and it's important to remember that the only person's worship we should be judging is our own.

I remember one time I was at a worship night with Jason Upton in Tulsa, Oklahoma. If you don't know of Jason Upton, I highly encourage you to check him out. As a worship leader myself, he has been one of the greatest influences in my life in regards to leading worship.

There was a crowd of around 1,000 or so and up until this point I had only heard Jason Upton's music. I hadn't been a part of a worship night with him, at least not in the kind of expressive environment that was present. The music began so I started worshiping God with the perfect amount of expression (not too reserved because I wasn't ashamed to worship Jesus but not too expressive because I wasn't one to try and bring attention to myself). The way I was worshiping was just right. Hopefully, you can detect the thick sarcasm I'm laying on. I was oozing with self-righteousness.

As I was perfectly worshiping the Lord, I opened my eyes and saw a guy down near the front who was dancing around wildly. I honestly wouldn't even call it dancing. It was more like he was flailing his body around in such a way that I knew he was just trying to bring attention to himself.

I tried to keep my mind and heart focused on the Lord as best as I could, but I couldn't stop looking at the guy who was distracting so many in worship. Why in the world was he doing that up at the very front? Why wouldn't he go to the back? I knew in my righteous judgment that the guy's heart was wrong and he needed to stop it. I then took it to the Lord because he needed to hear my case.

"Lord, look at him down there taking attention away from you. There's no way he's really worshiping you. He's trying to get attention for himself and be noticed by others. I can't believe this." And the last phrase I said to the Lord in this part of the conversation was, "Lord, there's no way he is worshiping you" to which the Holy Spirit quickly and lovingly responded, "And you are?"

My heart melted like wax. I was completely undone. His gentle and convicting words left me speechless. I had no response to give. No way of defending myself. The Lord spoke to me truth in love, and he had me cornered.

I broke down into tears. Those three simple words from the Holy Spirit did a massive transformational work in me. After that, I stopped judging other people's worship and ways of expression. It wasn't for me to judge and never should have been.

And I'd like to add that after many years of walking with the Lord, I'm now one of those "flailers." I don't have much rhythm or dance skills. I'm not afraid to admit it. But Psalm 149:3 doesn't say we are required to have these skills in order to dance before him! And the fact that the Bible says David danced before the Lord in an undignified way leaves the impression that he didn't have many skills either.

GIVE YOURSELF ROOM TO MAKE MISTAKES

This has been such a hard lesson for me. I'm not sure where I got it from but I struggled with finding my identity in my performance. For years as a worship leader, I determined if a worship service was successful by whether or not we made a mistake. If a mistake was made during a service, I would crumble inside. I couldn't get it off my mind the whole time. I'd leave service feeling frustrated and defeated.

I used to work as the graphic designer for a large billion dollar financial institution. Once I made a TV commercial that had a typo in it that didn't get caught before it was released. When someone tweeted about the error and insulted the company, I took it very personally. Certainly, it was a big mistake, but the shame and self-bullying that ensued were not healthy and were not the will of God for my life.

I used to think that in order for me to truly love God, I had to do it perfectly. If I ever made a mistake, I would be guilty of insincerely loving God. If it wasn't perfect, then I was a fake and a fraud. But God set me free from this mentality through the renewing of my mind by the true Word of God. He had to work out a lot of those half-truths that I let the enemy put in my mind.

When I realized that I didn't have to be perfect at loving him, I was then free to love him more sincerely and wholeheartedly than I ever had before. When I wasn't afraid of being rejected by him on any level in response to my mistakes, I stopped sitting on the sidelines in my walk with

Christ. I was free to run after him and accept myself and others in love even through the imperfections.

This truth set me free from one of the biggest mistakes of all - not loving him wholeheartedly. It's hard to accept, but when we are trying to love him perfectly, we're being motivated by fear of rejection and striving to not disappoint him. We are actually doing the thing we don't want to do - love him insincerely!

When we leave room for our mistakes and accept his mercy and grace as a constant need in our lives, we will actually be free to love him more sincerely and genuinely than we ever have before. We often think we have to be perfect at loving God in order to be sincere, but that's just not the truth. Yes, it's possible to be inauthentic in our love, but we need to leave room for grace in the process.

Let yourself dream and see visions of the Son of God. Don't overthink the things you see. Know that you are in process. Keep the Word of God in front of you and let it be your guide and firm foundation to stand on. You will learn many things along the way. The Holy Spirit will grow and develop your ability to see things in the Spirit. Just keep giving yourself grace along the way, because it's something he has for us in the process.

JESUS DID MANY THINGS THAT WE WOULD CONSIDER TO BE WEIRD

Sometimes the things of the Spirit can seem different, out of the ordinary, and even straight up weird. We need to give ourselves and others some room for the peculiar things of God. Let's look at some examples of works that Jesus did that if we saw today we'd think were weird.

Then Jesus spat on the ground and made some clay with his saliva. Then he anointed the blind man's eyes with the clay. And he said to the blind man, 'Now go and wash the clay from your eyes in the ritual pool of Siloam.' So he went and washed his face and as he came back, he could see for the first time in his life! (John 9:5-7, TPT)

So Jesus led him away from the crowd to a private spot. Then he stuck his fingers into the man's ears and placed some of his saliva on the man's tongue. Then he gazed into heaven, sighed deeply, and spoke to the man's ears and tongue, 'Ethpathakh,' which is Aramaic for 'Open up, now!' (Mark 7:33-34, TPT)

There are plenty of other stories in both the Old and New Testament alike that leave us wondering a little bit, but since we know the end of the stories, we see that they're not so weird after all. I'm not advocating that we go around and spit in people's eyes or on their tongues. I definitely would refrain from that, especially if you are new at hearing the voice of God or receiving visions from him.

However, as we are following the Holy Spirit, we need to be comfortable with the uncomfortable moments. Sometimes we hear him correctly and sometimes we don't. Sometimes we hear or get a vision from him and then act upon it in obedience, but we don't see the whole move of God come to completion. Perhaps the Lord wanted to use us in that moment and then continue to work his purpose through other means.

It's possible, for example, that the Lord would give us a vision in the Spirit of someone being healed or delivered. We go and tell that person what we received from the Spirit and afterward we may not see the result we expected at that moment. The man that Jesus healed of blindness by placing mud on his eyes didn't actually start seeing until he went and washed at the pool of Siloam.

However, when the results came to him, no one thought he was weird because it worked! When you are seeking the Lord and you receive something that stretches your thinking a bit, don't be afraid to do what he's asked. Know that the Lord is at work in the situation and that you have honored him through your obedience.

IT DOESN'T HAVE TO BE WEIRD
TO BE OF THE SPIRIT

On the other side of that, the things of the Spirit don't have to be strange or odd in nature. I feel that more often than not, the Holy Spirit moves through simple, common acts of obedience. It might be through simply giving a fellow believer a financial blessing because of what the Word says in Acts 4:32 (TPT). It says, "All the believers were one in mind and heart. Selfishness was not a part of their community, for they shared everything they had with one another."

Remember, John 6:63 tells us that his words are Spirit and life. When we simply respond to the Word of God, we can know that we are doing a very spiritual act of obedience.

Also, there will be many times that the Lord speaks to us or gives us a picture of something that isn't directly in the Bible word for word. For example, he may tell us to go to a grocery store and look for a specific person to tell him or her something the Lord puts on our hearts. This is called "rhema." Rhema is the Greek word for the personal Word of God spoken specifically to us.

Logos is the Greek word for the written Word of God. The example mentioned about blessing a believer in response to Acts 4:32 would be an example of logos. Logos and rhema are both considered the Word of God, just different expressions of it. Both of these forms of his Word are Spirit and life as John 6:63 tells us.

Either way, logos or rhema, it's important for us to know that the simple acts the Holy Spirit instructs us to do during communion with him don't have to be weird or complicated. Just simply listen, see, and trust that he is faithful in the process.

GAZING UPON JESUS ISN'T A NEW CONCEPT

The concept of gazing upon Jesus is not a newly discovered one. Not only is it Biblical, but it's something that the Church has experienced at different levels for many years now. Look at the words in the hymn "Turn Your Eyes Upon Jesus."

O soul, are you weary and troubled?
No light in the darkness you see?
There's light for a look at the Savior,
And life more abundant and free.

Turn your eyes upon Jesus,
Look full in his wonderful face,
And the things of earth will grow strangely dim,
In the light of his glory and grace.

Through death into life everlasting
He passed, and we follow him there;
O'er us sin no more hath dominion
For more than conquerors we are!

His Word shall not fail you, he promised;
Believe him and all will be well;

Then go to a world that is dying,
His perfect salvation to tell!

Don't be afraid to let your imagination run wild as you seek him in worship. As you pursue him in spirit and truth, open wide the gates of your inner being and let the Holy Spirit have his way. What have you got to lose? But the more important question is, what have you got to gain?

Keep yourself grounded in the Word of truth and pursue him in spirit. Don't get too caught up in trying to feel God. Don't worry if you don't feel the Holy Spirit goosebumps. This doesn't mean we should wonder if he is going to heal our emotions or not. We can be more than confident that he will.

He absolutely loves our feelings and emotions, and he places a high importance on caring for us at that place inside of us. He is the Shepherd of our souls and therefore he desires to care for our entire being (spirit, soul, and body). Just remember to seek him in spirit and truth. That's where the river of life starts to overflow into the other areas of our lives.

GOD'S DESIRE

It is the desire of the Lord that you experience all he has for you in this life. My hope is that you will be encouraged to seek the Lord in ways that you may have never thought were possible. I pray you have seen through the Word and revelation by the Holy Spirit that gazing upon Jesus is not just another one of our thoughts. When partnered with the Word and faith, it is a powerful and divine experience. It's an opportunity set before us that, if we choose to take advantage of, will keep the secret place burning with passion.

Just remember to seek him
in spirit and truth.
That's where the river of life
starts to overflow into
the other areas of our lives.

Beholding God in the beauty of his holiness is a radically life-changing experience and one that we Christians have unfortunately watered down or been afraid to explore. But no more.

We have been afraid of the things of the Spirit and we've sat on the sidelines far too long because of it. If the Church will embrace their God-given inheritance of seeing Jesus and beholding him in all his radiant light, then we will begin to reflect the majesty of who he is to the world.

Too many Christians have written the world off as hopeless. Yes, we know that there will be many people who reject Christ. However, there are many who are looking for him but just haven't had a witness come to him or her with the message of the gospel intoxicated by the fragrance of Christ that can only be found in the secret place.

We as Christians have focused too much on all the things we shouldn't do and focused so little on the glorious riches that are available through knowing Jesus personally. It's created a dead body of Christ in many ways. One that is bored in the place of prayer. This should not be, beloved! Isaiah 56:7 (ESV) says, "these I will bring to my holy mountain, and make them *joyful* in my house of prayer;"

He wants to exhilarate us in the place of prayer and our one-on-one communion with him. Let us, the Church, be filled to overflowing and spilling out the Spirit of God to all the world so that the entire earth will be filled with the knowledge of the glory of the Lord (Habakkuk 2:14).

I encourage and exhort you to seek out the fullness of joy that is found in his presence. The place that his Word says has pleasures forevermore. There is a wild, bliss-filled opportunity that lies before us and it can only be accessed through knowing Christ personally. Don't take it lightly or for granted. May our hearts echo the same prayer of Psalm 27:4 (TPT) which says,

Here's the one thing I crave from God, the one thing I seek above all else: I want the privilege of living with him every moment in his house, finding the sweet loveliness of his face, filled with awe, delighting in his glory and grace.

PRAYER & DECLARATION

I am excited for your future. I believe that your friendship with God is going to go deeper and your time with him will be overflowing with bliss, joy, and delight. To conclude this book, I encourage you to say this prayer and declaration:

Lord, thank you for the transforming work you are doing in my life. I praise you for opening my eyes to the glorious riches of knowing you. Thank you for helping me see you as Nathanael, Peter, James, and John did. You are correcting half-truths about your nature toward me in my mind. I am increasing in the knowledge of your grace, mercy, and love toward me. I am learning how to feast and commune with you in my spirit and it's feeding the rest of my entire being. Thank you for the great delight that you have in me. I get so excited about it that it makes me want to sneak away from the busyness of life so I can enjoy your presence. I love you, Jesus. I enjoy gazing upon your beauty and seeing the sweet loveliness of your face. In your wonderful name, amen.

REFLECTION

Spend some time reflecting on these questions. Use the space provided to journal and write down what the Holy Spirit is speaking to you.

1. Have you ever had a time that the Lord called you out like my experience at the Jason Upton event (pages 121-122)? If so, what did you learn from it?

2. Have you been too hard on yourself in regards to your relationship with God? If so, how do you see yourself walking in freedom with him?

3. God wants us (his house of prayer) and our times alone with him to be marked with joy (Isaiah 56:7). Write or draw how you envision your times with the Lord shifting this direction.

REFLECTION

Use the space provided below to write any personal revelations you've received. Write down words, phrases, or desires that are stirred within you. You can draw pictures that you may have seen in your mind while reading this chapter. This is a blank canvas to express your heart.

DON'T FORGET THESE THINGS

God wants to have delightful personal encounters with you often, just like he did with Jesus when he would withdraw from the crowds.

If you are a believer, you are a temple of the living God.

As a temple of God, you are made up of three separate but connected parts: spirit, soul, and body.

He dwells at the core of you in your spirit. Through communion with him in spirit and truth, the river of life will flow out of your spirit, into your soul, and then out of your body through acts of worship.

Time with God is foremost about heart-to-heart connection, not gaining knowledge.

You can gaze upon Jesus in spirit and truth, and through these encounters you will take on his nature (become like Christ).

Gazing upon him helps you develop a stronger relationship with him. It helps you remember that he isn't distant but is living within you.

Just like Jesus only did what he saw the Father do, so can you.

God desires witnessing to flow from our encounters with him in the secret place. He wants us to live inside out.

Witnessing should be an easy, natural overflow from seeing the transfigured Jesus, not a religious obligation.

You do not have to feel burdened or obligated by his desire to meet with you face-to-face. He is a friend and lover of our souls. He doesn't use pressure or frustration to manipulate us into nearness with him.

The Father takes great delight in you when you are at your best and when you are at your worst.

Anything that causes you to feel like you should distance yourself from God is not from God. No matter how true or valid it may seem, it's a lie.

Stop the self-bullying. Have grace, forgiveness, and patience for yourself just like he has towards you.

Self-imposed spiritual time-out from the presence of God is
not Biblical.

Approach his throne with boldness,
no matter what you've done.

Throw out the timer in your time with God.

Through the New Covenant promise made in Isaiah 54:9,
in Christ, God has no anger or wrath stored up for you.

The absence of sin doesn't create the presence of Jesus.
The presence of Jesus creates the absence of sin.

Obedience is not a prerequisite for communion.

You have a great, God-given imagination. He wants to paint
heavenly, truth-filled realities onto the canvas of your mind.

HAS THIS BOOK **HELPED** YOU
HAVE A MORE CONSISTENT,
VIBRANT, AND EXHILARATING
PRAYER LIFE?

IF SO, PLEASE **SHARE** WITH
OTHERS AND LET THEM
KNOW ABOUT THIS BOOK
SO THEY CAN **GROW** IN
THESE TRUTHS TOO!

HOW YOU CAN HELP
SPREAD THE MESSAGE...

WRITE A REVIEW ON AMAZON
(IF PURCHASED THERE)

*TELL US HOW BEHOLD HELPED
YOU BY EMAILING US AT
INFO@TABORPUBLISHING.COM*

*SHARE ABOUT THE BOOK
ON SOCIAL MEDIA*